Oregon Handbook
Wills and Estate Planning

Rees C. Johnson, Attorney

Hara PUBLISHING
Seattle, Washington

Hara Publishing
P.O. Box 19732
Seattle, Washington 98109
425-775-7868

Contents

Glossary **207**

Samples

Tables

Preface to Revised (Sixth) Edition

Contents of New Edition

This sixth edition reflects numerous changes in both federal and Oregon law since 1996, the date of publication of the fifth edition.

Education savings accounts, also known as Section 529 accounts, are a new way to fund post-secondary education expenses through state agencies. They are authorized by Congress and implemented by the states. Oregon and most other states in this country now authorize such accounts. Education savings accounts are described in Chapter 11.

The Economic Growth and Tax Relief Reconciliation Act of 2001, or EGTRRA for short, made substantial changes in the federal estate and gift tax laws. The major changes are explained in chapters 16 and 17.

New chapter 18 explains the income tax rules on adjustment in basis of capital assets when a person dies.

Note of Caution

This book, the author's newsletter and the author's website provide general legal and tax information about Oregon law and about federal law as it applies to Oregon residents. However, they cannot give you legal or tax advice on a specific matter or about laws of states other than Oregon. If you are seeking advice about a specific legal or tax matter, you should contact an attorney or tax expert and should not rely on this book, the author's newsletter or his website.

Introduction

The primary purpose of this book is to provide you with a practical guide to planning your estate and writing your will or living trust. It cannot and does not attempt to replace the services of estate planning professionals like lawyers and accountants, but it will give you a general understanding of estate planning and the legal and tax context in which it operates. It will make it easier for you to deal with and understand professional advisors when you do seek their help. This book also clears up a number of common misconceptions about estate planning and helps you avoid making planning mistakes.

A.   What Is Estate Planning?

To many people, estate planning means nothing more than having a will. They incorrectly assume that a will is all that is necessary to get their financial affairs in order, and that once it is signed they can file it away and forget about it.

While a will is central to many estates, for many individuals, a living trust has become the central document. Signing the documents, however, is merely one step in a process that starts with an analysis of your property and debts. This process may involve assistance from a number of different professional advisors, including a lawyer, an accountant, a trust officer, a life insurance agent, and an investment counselor.

Good estate planning means not only planning ahead so your affairs are in order when you die, but also planning today so that you can enjoy the maximum benefits from your property while you are alive.

Each estate plan should achieve the following goals:

(a) Preserve and build your wealth while you are alive and ensure financial security for yourself and your dependents;

(b) Maintain control of your property and affairs while you are alive;

(c) Minimize cost and delay in the transfer of your estate to your intended beneficiaries when you die;

(d) Minimize taxes, both while you are alive (income and gift taxes), and at your death (estate and inheritance taxes).

A poor estate plan can shrink the value of your assets and create unnecessary taxes, attorney fees, and delay. A good estate plan will prevent the transfer of your property and wealth to "laughing heirs," that is, distant relatives you never met or knew during your lifetime.

B.　The Estate Planning Process

A well-planned estate involves five steps.

1.　What Do You Own?

The first step is to make a list of all your property and debts. Include anything of value. You should try to value each item at current fair market value. This helps you estimate your taxes and income under various conditions.

Assemble and examine documents concerning property ownership, including deeds, mortgages, life insurance policies, investment records, and retirement programs.

2.　Who Are the Beneficiaries?

The second step is to analyze your present estate plan. If you have a will, check to see what property will pass under it and what will not. Check your life insurance policies to see who the beneficiaries are. You may discover that your estranged mother is the primary beneficiary, even though you have been married for 15 years and expect everything to go to your spouse. Or, if you are divorced, you may find that your ex-spouse still holds title to some of your assets.

3. Set Your Goals

Once you are sure that you know where you are, the next step is to set your goals. Make sure that you are getting maximum return on your investments at minimum tax cost. This includes providing sufficient cash funds to meet expenses at your death so that your property does not have to be sold at distress prices. Also make sure that your property will go to the intended beneficiaries and that steps are taken to minimize taxes.

4. Implement Your Goals

You already know that if you do not have a will, you need one. But you may also decide to change one or more of your investments, restructure ownership of certain assets, sign a trust agreement, or buy more life insurance. You might want to change beneficiaries, sign an advance directive, or make some lifetime gifts. These estate planning techniques are discussed more fully later in this book.

5. Review Your Plans

It is a good idea to schedule a periodic review of your estate plan, and to revise it, if necessary. Take a regular financial inventory and review all your estate planning documents to make certain that they are up to date and still reflect your goals. A good time to do an annual review is as of December 31, or after you receive all your year's investment reports, or when you prepare your income tax returns. You should also review your estate plan when there is a significant change in your family circumstances, in your wealth, or in the law.

Chapter 1

The Meaning of Probate and Nonprobate

To understand the role of a will or living trust and the function of probate procedure in estate planning, you must first understand the variety of ways in which property can be owned in Oregon and the significance of classifying property as probate or nonprobate.

This chapter defines some basic terms relating to estate planning and explains the difference between probate and nonprobate property. The next two chapters describe the ways you can own property in Oregon and how that property is transferred at death.

A. What the Words Mean

1. Estate

Your estate consists of all your property, both real and personal, including land, houses, furniture, personal belongings, checking and savings accounts, business interests, investments, life insurance, retirement benefits, and anything else you own of value.

It includes not only property you own and in which you have all the interest, such as fee title to real property, but also property in which you have a part interest because you own it jointly with someone else (e.g., property held jointly with right of survivorship), or property in which you have a limited interest, such as a life estate. All of these together constitute your estate.

2. Real and Personal Property

You may own both real and personal property. Real property is land and generally includes buildings and other fixtures that are permanent parts of the land.

Personal property includes all other property and can be divided into two categories: tangible personal property, such as furniture, clothing, and motor vehicles, and intangible personal property, such as stocks, bonds, bank accounts, life insurance, and contract rights.

3. Probate and Nonprobate Property

Your estate may consist of two types of property. The first type is property that is subject to probate administration. A good example is property in your own name, such as your home or other real property you own in fee title. Such property passes under your will and is subject to probate administration.

The other category of property is nonprobate property. Such property does not pass to another person under your will, and it is not subject to probate administration, either because your interest in it terminates on the date of your death and, therefore, there is nothing for you to give away, or because the property passes to some other designated person by law or by contract.

Common examples of nonprobate property are stocks and bonds that you own jointly with another person with right of survivorship and life insurance on your life in which you name a person, rather than your estate, as beneficiary. Property which is in a living trust at your death is another example of nonprobate property.

4. Probate Administration

Probate administration is a court-supervised procedure for transferring your probate property upon your death from your name to the persons who are legally entitled to it, either under the terms of your will or according to Oregon law.

It involves appointment of a personal representative, who is responsible for collecting all the property, paying all your creditors, paying expenses of administration, paying any taxes due, and distributing the property to the persons who are legally entitled to it.

The word "probate" generally refers to the manner in which a will's validity is established after someone has died. Administration of a deceased's estate generally refers to the court-supervised procedure for transferring the property, whether or not there is a will. For simplicity, the court procedure is described in this book as probate administration. Probate administration deals only with probate property. Nonprobate property is not subject to probate administration.

5. Will

A will is a legal document declaring your intentions concerning the disposition of your probate property after death. A will has no legal effect until it is admitted to probate (i.e., until its validity has been proven by proper court proceedings after the person making the will has died).

Most important, a will deals only with probate property. This does not mean that when you prepare your will you should ignore nonprobate property. For instance, if you own property jointly with right of survivorship, and you die first, the property will pass by law to the joint survivor and will not be subject to the terms of your will. However, if the other joint owner dies before you do, then you become the sole owner, what was nonprobate property becomes probate property and, if you do not change title, will pass under your will at your death. This possibility should be planned for and covered by your will.

The person making the will is known as the testator (if male) or testatrix (if female). He or she is described as dying testate (i.e., with a will).

6. Intestate Succession

A person who dies without a will is described as dying intestate. If you have probate property, it will be subject to probate administration regardless of whether or not you have a will.

If you do not have a will, the court will appoint a personal representative, and your property will pass to those persons known as your heirs, whom the law has designated to receive your probate property (see chapter 6). This law is called the law of intestate succession. It applies if you have no will or if, as sometimes happens, your will does not dispose of all your probate property.

B.   The Difference between Probate and Nonprobate Property

In Oregon there are two basic procedures for transferring ownership of property at death: probate and nonprobate. The procedure used depends on title or ownership of property at death. This rule is central to an understanding of estate planning in Oregon and to everything that follows in this book.

Probate property must go through probate in order to transfer ownership to the persons entitled to it. On the other hand, title to nonprobate property generally can be easily cleared when an owner dies. For example, assume that Michael died owning 250 shares of stock in a major national company. He owned 100 shares in his own name (a form of probate property) and 150 shares in joint and survivor ownership with his sister, Mary (a form of nonprobate property). His will left his entire estate to his brother, John. In order for John to get the 100 shares that are to go to him, Michael's estate would have to go through the probate procedure described later. Mary, on the other hand, would simply have to submit a few documents to a stock transfer agent to transfer the jointly owned 150 shares into her name alone.

If you die owning both probate and nonprobate property, your probate property must go through probate, but your nonprobate property does not. If you have a will, it determines who receives your probate property; if you do not have a will, Oregon's laws on intestate succession determine who receives your probate property.

If you have a will, however, it may dispose only of probate property and cannot determine who gets your nonprobate property. The manner in which you structure ownership of nonprobate property while you are alive will determine who receives that property. This occurs even if your will states something different. For instance, if you name your daughter as primary beneficiary of your IRA and she survives you, she will receive your IRA at your death, even though your will gives your

IRA to your son. Also, a will cannot change probate property into nonprobate property.

If you die with only nonprobate property, then your will has no legal significance. It is not admitted to probate or filed with the court or any other public authority. This does not mean, however, that if you have only nonprobate property, you do not need a will. Property that is nonprobate now may become probate property prior to your death.

C.   Some Property can be Either Probate or Nonprobate

Several types of property are not easily cataloged as either probate or nonprobate. These include life insurance and other contract property, business interests, and property that does not typically have documents of title, such as bearer bonds and certain tangible personal property.

1. Life Insurance

If you own life insurance and name a beneficiary other than your estate, such as your spouse, and the beneficiary survives you, the proceeds will go to that person and will not be probate property. However, if you name your estate as the beneficiary, or if all your named beneficiaries die before you do, then the proceeds will be part of your estate and, therefore, probate property.

Some life insurance agents recommend that a husband own the policies on his wife's life and the wife own the policies on her husband's life. However, except in rare cases, cross ownership for life insurance policies accomplishes little. For example, Joan and Bob are married and each owns a policy on the other's life. If Joan dies first, the policy that Joan owned on Bob's life will have to go through probate. And if a couple owning policies on each others' lives decide to divorce, the cross ownership will complicate their financial matters.

2. Other Contract Property

Several kinds of contractual property normally do not become probate property because there is a named surviving beneficiary, but may become probate property because of the terms of the contract. Typical examples are:

(a) death benefits or annuities payable under retirement, pension, and profit-sharing plans and individual retirement accounts (IRAs);

(b) deferred compensation and other employer-provided death benefits;

(c) buy-sell arrangements for small businesses;

(d) credit union share accounts with named beneficiaries; and

(e) payable on death (POD), transfer on death (TOD), and "in trust for" (IT) accounts at financial institutions.

3. Businesses

If you are in business for yourself, your interest in the business may be either as a sole proprietor, a partner in a partnership, a shareholder in a corporation, or a member in a limited liability company. Your ownership interest in each type of business may be probate or nonprobate property, depending on how you structure ownership.

a. Sole Proprietorship

A sole proprietorship is a business owned by one person. The assets of a sole proprietorship are probate property, and each asset (such as a vehicle, equipment, or inventory) is a separate asset of the probate estate.

b. Partnership

A partnership is an association of two or more persons to carry on a business for profit as co-owners. A general partnership is usually established by written agreement, but it can exist by a verbal agreement. A limited partnership must be in writing and filed with the state.

In a general partnership, all the partners are liable for partnership obligations and have a voice in partnership decisions. In a limited partnership, one or more partners, known as limited partners, are not liable for the partnership obligations, but are only liable to make any agreed-upon contribution to the partnership. A limited partner is generally a passive investor and has little or no say in the business. A joint venture is a partnership, general or limited, for a specific, one-time business venture, such as developing and selling a parcel of real property.A partner's interest is probate property unless the partnership agreement converts that interest into nonprobate property either by making the surviving spouse or some other person the successor in interest to the deceased partner or by making the partnership interest a form of joint and survivorship property.

c. Corporation

A corporation is an artificial, separate, legal entity created by articles of incorporation. The shareholders own the business, and their ownership interest is reflected in stock certificates. Stock in a corporation may be held in either probate or nonprobate forms of property.

d. Limited Liability Company

A limited liability company, or LLC, is a flexible form of business entity, which can be designed to combine the limited liability protection of a corporation with the income tax treatment of a partnership. A member's interest in an LLC can be held in either probate or nonprobate forms of property.

4. Property without Documents of Title

Normally, it is easy to tell whether property is probate or nonprobate because there is a deed, certificate, or other document of title which indicates the form of ownership. However, some types of property do not have documents of title and may require special planning to minimize disputes over ownership when a person dies.

Two major types of such property are most tangible personal property (such as works of art and coin and stamp collections) and bearer bonds (which are bonds not registered in the name of the owner). A bearer bond may be redeemed by the person possessing it. Bearer bonds should be mentioned in your will and in any inventory of your property.

Tangible personal property can create problems in second marriages. Suppose each spouse brings certain furniture to a second marriage. They each intend that when the first spouse dies, the surviving spouse will have use of the furniture of the deceased spouse until his or her own death, at which time it is to go back to the children of the spouse that died first. One way to avoid a fight between the two sets of children after both spouses have died is to have a written agreement that identifies each spouse's separate property and states what is to happen upon the death of each spouse (see chapter 10).

Finally, there is a category of property over which you may have control while you are alive, but which you may not have power to dispose of at your death, because you do not own the property. This includes any property that you hold in a fiduciary capacity, such as trustee, guardian, conservator, or custodian, or that you hold as agent for someone else.

If you rent a safe deposit box in a bank in the names of two or more persons as joint tenants, it does not make the contents of the box joint property. The joint tenants could have an agreement making the contents joint property. This might make sense for contents without documents of title, such as a stamp or coin collection, or jewelry.

Chapter 2

Probate Property

This chapter describes the most common examples of property subject to probate administration and also subject to disposition by your will.

A. Sole Ownership

Any property that you own in your own name (and not jointly with any other person) and that has no type of limitation in terms of years or otherwise (such as a life estate) is your sole property and constitutes probate property.

For instance, if you own real property and the deed lists you as the sole grantee and does not put any limitations on the nature of the property interests granted to you, then you own that property in fee simple or fee title, and it passes as probate property.

B. Tenancy in Common

Tenancy in common is a form of joint ownership involving two or more persons, each owning an undivided interest in the property. Real property is frequently owned this way. For instance, a deed may read "to John Doe and Peter Smith, each an undivided one-half interest, as tenants in common."

Upon the death of a tenant in common, the deceased tenant's share passes according to his or her will, and is subject to probate administration. If there is no will, the share is subject to the laws of

13

intestate succession. It does not automatically pass to the surviving tenant in common.

The most obvious example of a tenancy in common is an express conveyance or deed of real property containing the required language. However, there are several situations involving property transactions that may create a tenancy in common without any express language.

1. Inheritances and Devises

If property passes through probate administration and is distributable to more than one person, it is generally distributed to those persons as tenants in common. This may occur, for instance, when a brother and sister inherit real property from a parent and own it as tenants in common.

2. Personal Property Owned by Spouses

If you are married, it may surprise you to learn that you may own some of your personal property with your spouse as tenants in common and not as joint tenants with any right of survivorship.

Under Oregon law, it is presumed that personal property is owned by spouses as tenants in common unless there is some express agreement providing for some other form of tenancy that clearly indicates survivorship. Express agreements of this kind can be made for any personal property, such as stocks and bonds or motor vehicles where there is a document of title. A stock certificate or motor vehicle certificate of title can, and usually does, expressly state that the property is owned jointly with right of survivorship.

Tangible personal property, such as furniture, furnishings, personal belongings, antiques, works of art, coin collections, and jewelry, does not have documents of title. If you and your spouse own it jointly, you own it as tenants in common.

If the wills of both you and your spouse provide that at the death of one spouse all property belongs to the other spouse, then there is no problem with this type of ownership. Nor is it a problem if there is total family harmony and your children assume and expect that your husband or wife will get all your jointly-owned personal property when you die. But this is not always the case. If you die intestate leaving children from a previous marriage as well as a surviving spouse, your spouse will receive only one-half of your share of the personal property and your children of the earlier marriage will be entitled to the other half.

The same problem can occur if you and your spouse lend someone money. Suppose the person to whom you loaned the money made a note payable to John and Jane Doe, husband and wife. The right to the proceeds from repayment of the loan is a tenancy in common. When one of the spouses dies, that spouse's one-half interest would pass as probate property.

A survivorship interest in the proceeds from the promissory note could be accomplished with either of the following two phrases: "John and Jane Doe, husband and wife, as joint tenants with right of survivorship" or "John and Jane Doe take the proceeds, not as tenants in common, but with right of survivorship, that is, upon the death of the spouse first to die, the surviving spouse shall be entitled to all proceeds."

3. Real Property Owned by Divorced Spouses

If a married couple owns real property as tenants by the entirety (see chapter 3) and continue to own the property jointly after divorce, either because the divorce decree does not deal with the property rights of each of the parties or because it directed that each shall have an interest in the property, the tenancy by the entirety is converted into a tenancy in common.

4. Invalid Marriage

A man and woman who either think they are validly married or present themselves as validly married, but in fact are not, will be treated as owning any jointly owned property as tenants in common, even though a deed or contract of purchase may list them as husband and wife.

In one case, Fred and Rosemary were married and property was deeded to them as Fred and Rosemary, husband and wife. Normally this would create a tenancy by the entirety, which means that when Fred died, the property would belong outright to Rosemary. Unfortunately for Rosemary, she and Fred were first cousins, and under Oregon law, marriages between first cousins are void. Fred died, and Fred's daughter, Fidelia, filed a lawsuit claiming that she was entitled to Fred's one-half interest as a tenant in common with Rosemary. The court agreed.

5. What You Should Know About a Tenancy in Common

There are a number of important points to consider about a tenancy in common.

(a) Property may be owned in unequal shares. A deed creating a tenancy in common might read:

> To John Doe, an undivided one-third interest, and to
> Peter Smith, an undivided two-thirds interest, as tenants in
> common.

(b) There may be more than two co-owners. There is no legal limit to the number, but there are practical limits to consider.

(c) You can have a different form of ownership on top of the tenancy in common. For example, if two couples purchase a beach house together, each couple owns its half interest as tenants in common. But each couple can also own its half interest as tenants by the entirety with each other. The deed might read:

> To John Doe and Mary Doe, husband and wife, as
> tenants by the entirety of an undivided one-half interest, and
> Peter Smith and Betty Smith, husband and wife, as tenants by
> the entirety of an undivided one-half interest, as tenants in
> common.

If John dies first, Mary would come into sole title of their one-half interest. When Mary dies, her one-half interest becomes probate property.

(d) Each share may be sold, mortgaged, given away, left in a will, or seized by creditors of the owner of the share without affecting the rights of the other co-owner and without his or her consent.

(e) Each co-owner is entitled to possession of the entire property, but not to the exclusion of the other co-owner. For example, when the Does purchased their one-half interest in the beach house, they did not buy just the left half. They own the whole house jointly with the Smiths.

(f) If one co-owner pays for necessary repairs, property taxes, insurance premiums, or liens and encumbrances on the property, he or she may claim reimbursement from the other co-owner. This is not true for the cost of improvements to the property that the other co-owner has not agreed to.

(g) If one co-owner receives rent or other income from the property, he or she has to account to the other co-owner.

(h) If one co-owner reduces the value of the property without the consent of the other, he or she is liable for that share of the loss of value.

(i) If the co-owners cannot get along, the property can be partitioned by court action. If the property can be physically divided without reducing its value, the court will do so. Otherwise, the court will direct the property to be sold and the proceeds to be divided between the co-owners.

(j) Co-owners can enter a written agreement amending and protecting their interests in the property. This is advisable especially for co-owners of rental or investment property. A tenancy in common agreement typically limits the right of one co-owner to transfer or encumber that co-owners' interest in the property without the consent of the other co-owner, and directs who will manage the property and how income and expenses will be handled.

C. Remainder Interest

It is possible for two persons to have successive interests in property. For instance, in your will you could leave a piece of real property to two people: to one person for life, who then has what is known as a life tenancy with the right to use the property for his or her lifetime; and then to another person, whose interest begins upon the life tenant's death, and who has what is known as a remainder interest.

In this case, the person who has the remainder interest has a present legal interest in the property subject to probate administration, even though he or she does not have a present right to possess the property and may never possess the property if he or she dies before the life tenant.

If the person with the remainder interest, the remainderman, dies before the life tenant, then the heirs or the persons named in the remainderman's will are entitled to possession of the property when the life tenant dies.

Although this occurs most commonly with real property, it also can be used with personal property. A remainder interest can be given as a lifetime transfer through a deed or in a person's will. A provision in a will might state:

> I give a life estate in X property to Jane Doe, and upon her death, I give the remainder to John Doe.

A typical lifetime deed may involve giving a remainder interest and reserving a life estate. It could read:

> John Doe, Grantor, conveys to Jane Doe all that real property situated in Multnomah County, Oregon, reserving unto Grantor a life estate for the term of the Grantor's life.

D. Inheritance, Devise, or Trust Distribution

If you are an heir of a relative who has died leaving probate property and no will, or if you are a devisee under that person's will, you have a legally recognized interest in that relative's property as of the date of that relative's death. If you die before you receive that property, your interest is subject to probate administration.

Similarly, if you are the beneficiary of a revocable living trust, and the trustor has died, you have a legally recognized interest in the trustor's property as of the date of the trustor's death. If you die after the trustor but before you receive distribution, your interest in the trust is subject to probate administration.

E. Other Probate Property

There is a category of property in which a deceased person may have no interest or title of record at the time of death, but which may nevertheless end up as probate property. This can happen, for example, if the decedent was incapacitated shortly prior to death and transferred all assets to another person, but the transfer is declared invalid because of the improper influence of the other person or because of the mental incapacity of the deceased. In that case, the personal representative of the estate can compel the other person to transfer those assets into the estate where they will be considered probate property.

Animals, such as farm animals or race horses, are probate property. However, an animal worth less than $2,500 kept by a person as a pet is not considered probate property and need not be listed in the inventory of a probate estate. Any family member, friend or animal shelter may take custody of a pet on the pet owner's death.

Finally, assets that may not be probate property at the time you write a will may end up probate property at the time of your death. An obvious example is property which you own jointly with right of survivorship with some other person, and that other person dies before you do. Or you may own life insurance on your life designating certain beneficiaries, all of whom die before you do. In that event, the life insurance proceeds would become part of your estate and constitute probate property.

F.   Community Property

Property that would normally be considered probate property, but which you acquired with proceeds from the sale of property previously acquired as a married person in a community property state, may not be subject to probate administration in its entirety. Oregon is a common law state, which means that the rights of spouses to property are determined by the English common law tradition. The community property system, which has a different set of rules concerning the rights of spouses to marital assets, is derived from the Spanish tradition through Louisiana.

Oregon is surrounded by community property states (California, Idaho, Nevada, and Washington). There are also four other states that follow the community property tradition (Arizona, Louisiana, New Mexico, and Texas). It is not uncommon, therefore, for married couples who acquire property in community property states to move to Oregon.

Under Oregon law, any property you and your spouse acquired while married and living in a community property state retains its community property characteristics even if you sell the property in the community property state and purchase property in Oregon in your own name. If you were to die under those circumstances, one-half of your property would automatically belong to your surviving spouse even though the property is in your own name alone and would normally be subject to probate administration in its entirety. The other half would be subject to probate administration and disposition under your will. An express agreement between you and your spouse is needed if you want to change this result.

Community property law will also determine how you own real property in a community property state, even if you are an Oregon resident. For instance, if you own a beach house in Washington jointly with your spouse, a half interest in the property will belong to your spouse when you die, and the other half will be probate property. If you want the entire interest to pass to your spouse by right of survivorship, as would happen in Oregon with tenancy by the entirety, you and your spouse must sign and record a community property agreement.

Chapter 3

Nonprobate Property

Nonprobate property does not pass under your will or under the laws of intestate succession. The most common type of nonprobate property is property owned jointly or concurrently by two or more persons with right of survivorship. That is, upon the death of the first co-owner, title automatically vests in the surviving co-owner.

Tenancies by the entirety, joint tenancies with right of survivorship in real property, and most joint tenancies with right of survivorship in personal property have similar attributes.

(a) Each co-owner is entitled to one-half of the rents and profits.

(b) Neither co-owner can force a severance or division of their joint interest in the property. That is, one owner cannot convert it into a tenancy in common by conveying the interest in the property to a third person. The one exception is joint tenancies in personal property created after 1974, where this right of severance does exist.

(c) Either co-owner can convey or encumber his or her own interest. However, all the grantee or creditor gets is an undivided interest subject to the right of survivorship in the other co-owner. This means if the other co-owner outlives the co-owner conveying the property, the grantee or creditor gets nothing.

These rules do not apply to joint bank accounts, which are discussed in section **G**.

A. Tenancy by the Entirety

Tenancy by the entirety is a unique form of joint ownership of real property owned by a married couple. Under a tenancy by the entirety, upon the death of the spouse first to die, the property belongs solely to the surviving spouse.

Contrary to the presumption of tenancy in common in personal property (see chapter 2), real property owned by spouses jointly is presumed to be owned as tenants by the entirety. Thus, a deed conveying property to John and Jane Doe, husband and wife, creates a tenancy by the entirety. This also applies to contracts to purchase real property in which the purchasers are husband and wife. A section in the contract stating that the purchasers are husband and wife is sufficient to create a tenancy by the entirety.

The one critical element of a tenancy by the entirety is that the parties are married to each other. If they are not married or if the marriage is invalid, they will own their real property as tenants in common.

B. Other Survivorship — Real Property

Persons not married to each other may own real property jointly with the right of survivorship. This form of ownership is not limited to two persons; it could be three or more persons, all owning interests in the property, with the property finally belonging to the last of the joint owners to die.

The language in deeds or contracts to purchase that establishes this ownership may be of two different types. It may read as follows:

> John Doe, Ronald Doe, and George Doe, not as tenants
> in common, but with right of survivorship, that is, the fee
> shall vest in the survivor of the grantees.

A second type of language would be as follows:

> John Doe, Robert Doe, and Ron Doe, as joint tenants
> with right of survivorship and not as tenants in common.

C. Survivorship — Personal Property

It is also possible for a married couple, or two or more persons, whether or not related, to hold personal property — tangible and intangible — jointly with right of survivorship. Generally, however, express language on the document of title must be used to create such an interest. Thus, if two or more persons wish to own a car jointly with right of survivorship, survivorship language must appear on the certificate of title issued by the Motor Vehicle Division. Similarly, if stocks or bonds are to be held jointly with right of survivorship, that language, typically the initials JTWROS, must expressly appear on the certificates.

There are two closely related forms of joint and survivorship ownership in Oregon with respect to personal property. One is known simply as joint tenancy and the other is generally called joint tenancy with right of survivorship. There is no difference between the two forms of joint ownership with respect to the survivor's right to sole ownership when the first joint owner dies.

The only significant difference between the two forms of ownership is that with a joint tenancy, one joint owner can sell or otherwise transfer his or her interest without the consent of the other joint owner. In property held jointly with right of survivorship, this is not possible.

D. Seller-Financed Real Property Sales

Seller-financed real property installment sales are an exception to the general rule that express language is needed to create a survivorship interest in jointly-owned personal property. The seller's interest in a real estate contract or a note secured by a trust deed or mortgage is considered personal property because the seller's sole interest is the right to receive the balance of the purchase price. Seller-financed real property sales are in two forms: an installment real estate contract, in which the seller retains title as security until the purchase price is paid, or a conveyance of title upon sale in exchange for an installment promissory note for all or part of the purchase price secured by a mortgage or trust deed against the property.

Under Oregon law, owners of real property who own it either as tenants by the entirety or in some other form of survivorship ownership may sell it on an installment basis. If one joint owner dies before the purchase price is paid in full, the other joint owner is considered to have the right to receive payments of all the deferred installments of the purchase price by right of survivorship. The estate of the deceased joint owner has no claim to the payments. No language of survivorship need appear in the contract, note, trust deed, or mortgage.

E.   U.S. Government Securities

Joint ownership of securities issued by the U.S. government is a second exception to the general rule requiring express language to create a survivorship interest in jointly-owned property. For instance, Series EE and HH Savings bonds can be owned in joint and survivorship ownership simply by listing the two owners' names with the word "or" between them. Savings bonds cannot be owned by joint owners as tenants in common.

Treasury Direct accounts, through which you can purchase Treasury bills, notes, and bonds, can be owned as tenants in common and in two forms of joint and survivorship ownership. One form, called "joint ownership with right of survivorship," requires registration in the names of two individuals, joined by the word "and" and ending with "right of survivorship." Transaction requests must be signed by both owners. This form of registration creates a conclusive right of survivorship.

The other form, called "co-ownership," requires registration in the names of two individuals, joined by the word "or." Transaction requests may be signed by either co-owner. This form of registration creates a conclusive right of survivorship, without any reference to survivorship.

F.   Life Estates and Remainders

A life estate and remainder is a common planning tool in small estates where the home is the major asset. For example, it might be attractive to a widow who has a home and few other assets to leave everything to her adult son. In order to put her affairs in order and to avoid probate, she could convey title to her house to her son and reserve a life estate for the remainder of her life. When she dies, the right to possess the property automatically goes to her son as the remainderman without probate administration.

The widow's conveyance of a remainder interest to her son gives the son a part of the ownership of the house while his mother is still alive. However, the widow has exclusive right to the possession of the house for the rest of her life. When she dies, her son is entitled to possession. All he has to do to clear his mother's name from the title is to record a copy of her death certificate in the deed records of the county where the property is located. No probate of the widow's life estate is necessary.

This sounds like good estate planning, but there are a number of disadvantages to life estates and remainders. Consider the following:

(a) The widow cannot sell or mortgage the house without her son's consent. If there were a falling out between the two and the son refused consent, the widow would be trapped with the house.

(b) If the son dies before his mother, the son's remainder interest becomes probate property of his estate and passes to his beneficiaries either by the terms of his will or by intestate succession. The widow may find that she may have ownership of her house with someone she doesn't even know!

(c) If the widow changes her mind about her estate plan and wants to leave the house to someone else, she will have to persuade her son to deed the remainder interest back to her.

(d) If the son goes through a divorce, his remainder interest would be considered when assets are divided with his wife. It is unlikely, but not impossible, that the ex-wife could end up owning the remainder interest.

(e) The widow would not be entitled to the property tax deferral for persons age 62 or older.

(f) Life estate-remainder relationships create a number of obligations between the widow and son. The widow, as life tenant, is responsible for repairs to the property to ensure it does not decline in value. She is required to pay the interest and the remainder of the principal on any mortgages on the house. She is also required to pay fire insurance premiums and property taxes on the home.

(g) If the widow and son decide to sell the house, each would be entitled to a share of the net sales proceeds. The widow's share may qualify for the $250,000 exclusion from capital gains tax, but the son's share would not.

(h) Creation of a remainder interest constitutes a gift for gift tax purposes (unless the son bought the remainder interest) and the widow may have to file a gift tax return and to pay gift taxes.

Life estates and remainders should be used with caution. If you want to give a son or daughter a remainder interest in your home while you are alive, make sure that you understand how much control of your home you are giving up. Even if there is a strong bond of mutual trust, you would be wise to prepare a written agreement outlining the rights and duties of you as the life tenant and your child as the remainderman.

You can also provide in your will that at your death you will give a life estate in your home to one person and the remainder interest to another. Or, because of the rigid rules that govern life estates and remainders, you might want to put the home in trust, directing the trustee to permit the life tenant to live there for life and distribute the remainder at the life tenant's death.

G. Joint Bank Accounts

A joint account is a deposit account with a financial institution payable on request to one of two or more persons. Checking accounts, savings accounts, certificates of deposit, and share accounts can all be owned as joint accounts. A financial institution includes commercial banks, savings and loan associations and credit unions.

1. Features of Joint Accounts

A unique feature of a joint account is that one party to the account can withdraw funds from the account without the knowledge or consent of the other party. This unique feature accounts both for the popularity and for the drawbacks of the joint account. Most other types of joint ownership assets require the consent and signature of all owners for a withdrawal or any other significant action relating to the asset.

Here are the basic rules relating to joint accounts:

(a) Joint accounts may be owned by two or more persons.

(b) During the lifetimes of all the parties, the joint account belongs to them in proportion to their net contributions to the sums on deposit. The net contribution of a party means the sums of all deposits of that party, less withdrawals by the party which have not been paid to the other party, plus a pro rata share of the interest.

(c) Sums on deposit in a joint account may be paid by the financial institution to any one or more of the parties to the account without the knowledge or consent of the other party and without regard to whether the other party is incapacitated or deceased.

(d) Sums remaining on deposit at the death of the party first to die belong by right of survivorship to the surviving party as against the estate of the deceased party. The only exceptions are if there is clear and convincing evidence of a different intent on record with the financial institution at the time of death or if the deceased party is the last surviving party.

(e) So long as the financial institution pays funds to one of the parties to the account, it is discharged from all claims for the amounts paid, regardless of the actual ownership of the funds in the account. The only exception is if the financial institution receives written notice from one of the parties not to permit withdrawals by the other party.

2. Risks of Joint Accounts

Joint accounts are popular because they are convenient to set up and to use. They are appropriate for married couples with stable marriages. It is common for a widow or widower to set up a joint account with a child in order to enable the child to pay the parent's bills in case the parent becomes incapacitated. Frequently a parent does so without understanding the consequences.

(a) The parent may not realize that by adding the child's name to the account, she is converting the account from a probate asset to a nonprobate asset. Assume that a parent has two children, a son and a daughter, a will that states that at the parent's death, the estate will be divided equally between the children, and that the parent owns a joint account with the daughter. At the parent's death, the daughter will receive all the funds in the joint account (with no duty to share them with her brother) plus half of the property which passed under the will.

(b) The parent may not realize that the child has an apparent ownership interest in the account which creditors or an ex-spouse may try to reach. In one Oregon case, this happened to a married couple, Corrine and Roy. Corrine had incurred a debt prior to her marriage to Roy. After they married, they set up a joint bank account with some of Roy's funds. Corrine's creditors obtained a judgment against Corrine and garnished the account; that is, obtained the funds in the account by legal procedure. Roy proved that he had contributed all the funds, so Corrine's creditors got nothing from the account. But Roy had to go through both a trial court and an appellate hearing before the case was resolved in his favor.

(c) The IRS may also try to reach funds in a joint account. If the IRS levies a joint account, the financial institution may delay surrender of the funds for 21 days. This gives the parties to the joint account time to notify the IRS of errors concerning the levy or ownership of the funds.

(d) Because of the unique ability of either joint owner to withdraw the funds from a joint bank account, temptation to abuse the trust placed in the non-depositor joint owner is great. In one case, John put money in a joint bank account with his son, Jim. Without John's consent, Jim took the money out and used it as a down payment on an apartment which he purchased in his and his wife's name. John got his money back from his son, but again he had to go to court.

3. Avoiding Joint Account Problems

There are several steps you can take to minimize the risks that can occur with joint accounts.

(a) If your sole purpose is to give a person funds in an account upon your death without probate, use a revocable trust (ITF) account or a payable-on-death (POD) account. (See section H.) With this kind of account, you have sole control of the funds while you are alive, but upon your death, the funds belong to the beneficiary you designate without probate of your estate.

(b) If you want to give a person funds in an account at the time of your death and also have that person able to use those funds for your benefit if you become ill or incapacitated, but for no other purpose, you can use a joint account. However, you should also have a written agreement, signed by both you and the other joint owner, which states when and for what purposes the other joint owner may withdraw funds while you are alive, and also what he or she is to do with the funds when you die. Of course, if you keep the checkbook, passbook, or time certificate, this will give you some practical protection; such protection is not available with a statement account.

(c) If your sole purpose is to have someone pay your bills while you are ill or incapacitated, and you want the funds to pass under your will and be subject to probate, use an account in your name alone, but give someone else a limited power of attorney to withdraw funds for your benefit. Most financial institutions have signature cards for this purpose. You should also have an agreement with that person concerning when and for what purposes the funds may be withdrawn.

(d) Whatever type of account you select, study the signature card and make certain you know what it says before you sign.

H. Living Trusts and POD Property

The interest of a trustor under a living trust is nonprobate property. In the typical living trust, you as trustor will transfer title to all your probate property to a bank or individual as trustee with instructions contained in a written trust agreement requiring the trustee to deal with your property as you direct for the remainder of your life. When you die, the trustee who has title to your property will distribute your property according to the terms of the trust agreement and without probate. Living trusts are discussed in more detail in chapter 5.

Another type of living trust is the so-called "totten" trust or ITF (in trust for) deposit account, available at many financial institutions. This is a form of ownership of deposit accounts where you name yourself as trustee of the funds on deposit and have unrestricted use of the funds while you are alive, but at your death the financial institution distributes the proceeds to the beneficiary whom you have named on the signature card.

Payable-on-death (POD) deposit accounts are identical to totten trusts, but use different words to describe the parties. On POD accounts you are described as the owner rather than the trustee and have all rights of ownership while you are alive. When you die, the financial institution distributes the funds to the named payee or beneficiary.

United States savings bonds can also be owned on a POD basis. One significant difference from POD deposit accounts, however, is that you, as owner, may cash in a bond without the beneficiary's consent, but you cannot remove the beneficiary's name without consent.

Under the Uniform TOD ("transfer on death") Security Registration Act, you may register stocks, bonds, and other securities with beneficiary designations, similar to POD deposit accounts.

If one person owns a security and wants to name one beneficiary, the security is registered: "John S. Brown TOD ("transfer on death") or POD ("pay on death") John S. Brown, Jr."

If two persons own a security and want to designate a beneficiary after both have died, the security is registered: "John S. Brown and Mary B. Brown JT TEN ("joint tenants with right of survivorship") TOD John S. Brown, Jr."

It is also possible and advisable to name contingent beneficiaries to take the security in the event the primary beneficiary fails to survive you.

Brokerage accounts as well as individual securities can be owned in TOD and POD forms of ownership. However, the law does not require the registering entity to register securities in beneficiary form, and it permits the registering entity to establish the terms, conditions, and form of such registration. If you are interested in beneficiary registration for any of your securities, you must first check with your stockbroker if it is your brokerage account, or the issuing company or its transfer agent for individual securities, to see if they permit such registration.

Because POD and TOD property passes to a named beneficiary at the owner's death, it does not go through probate. However, like life insurance and other contract property, if all named beneficiaries predecease you, then this type of property can become probate property at your death.

Chapter 4

Introduction to Trusts

A trust is one of the most versatile and widely used estate planning tools. This chapter describes the general rules which apply to all trusts. The next chapter discusses the revocable living trust, one of the most popular trusts.

A trust is a three-way arrangement where one person transfers title to property to another person who holds and manages it for the benefit of a third person.

The property placed in the trust is known variously as the assets, the trust estate, the principal, the *corpus*, or the *trust res*. It is important to distinguish between the principal and income of the trust. The principal of the trust is the property of the trust as it may change in type through sale, purchase, and reinvestment. The income is the earnings from the principal, such as interest, dividends, and rent.

A. Trustor, Trustee, and Beneficiary

The trustor is the person setting up the trust and whose property is placed in trust. This person is also called the settlor or grantor.

The trustee is the person who takes legal title to the trust property and manages it for the benefit of another person. The trustee may be an individual, a bank or other financial institution authorized by state law to engage in trust business, or, occasionally, a charitable organization. More than one trustee, or co-trustees, may act at the same time.

The beneficiary is the person for whom the trust is managed. There can be more than one beneficiary and there may be classes of beneficiaries, such as children or grandchildren. There can be successive beneficiaries as well. For example, a child may receive benefits for all of his or her life after which one or more grandchildren start receiving benefits from the trust.

Some beneficiaries may be entitled to only the income of the trust. Others may be entitled to only the principal, and still others, to both.

B.   Categories of Trusts

There are two broad categories of trusts — living trusts (sometimes called *inter vivos* trusts), and testamentary trusts. You establish a living trust during your lifetime by a trust agreement which you and the trustee sign. You usually "fund" or transfer assets to the trustee during your lifetime.

There are two categories of living trusts, revocable and irrevocable. You can revoke or amend a revocable living trust, so long as you are alive and competent. The primary purposes of a revocable living trust are to avoid probate and plan for your incapacity. You cannot amend or revoke an irrevocable living trust. Irrevocable living trusts are used primarily for various tax purposes.

A testamentary trust comes into existence after you die and can be either in your will or in the post-death part of your revocable living trust. An example of a testamentary trust is a trust you establish to provide for the education of your children or grandchildren after you die.

C.   Anatomy of a Trust

The trust document will typically contain the following:

(a) A description of the property being placed in the trust.

(b) Identification of the beneficiaries by name or by class and a description of the beneficiaries' rights under the trust.

(c) The details on how long the trust will last. One of the advantages of a trust is that you can control how the property is managed and spent for one or more generations after your death. By law, however, a trust can continue only for the duration of the lives of the beneficiaries who are alive at the trustor's death, plus 21 years, or 90 years after the trustor's death, whichever is later.

(d) The name of the trustee. Alternative trustees can be named if the trustee fails to accept, dies, resigns, or is incapacitated.

(e) Guidelines for distribution to beneficiaries. For example, the trust may require regular distribution of income or it may require discretionary distribution based on a standard such as support, education, or medical needs.

(f) The powers of beneficiaries. It may give a beneficiary power to withdraw part of the principal out of the trust each year. This is in effect a power to order the trustee to distribute part of the principal to the beneficiary. A beneficiary may also have a power of appointment. For example, suppose you set up a trust naming your spouse as the income beneficiary and you want the principal to go to your children after your spouse's death. You can provide that the principal will go to your children but give your spouse a power of appointment to determine how much each child will receive. This power normally would be exercised in your spouse's will. The beneficiary who is given the power of appointment is called the donee or the holder of the power. The person to whom the property is appointed by the donee is known as the appointee. The trust agreement will state who receives the property if the donee fails to exercise the power of appointment. Such a person is known as the taker in default.

(g) Directions to the trustee regarding investment of the trust assets. It usually gives the trustee discretionary power on how to invest, but it may list certain types of investments only, or it may direct the trustee to use certain investment counselors to determine how to make investments.

(h) Outline of trustee's powers. Generally a trustee is given all the powers necessary to carry out the terms of the trust. In Oregon, the Uniform Trustee's Powers Act applies to all trusts unless otherwise stated in the trust.

(i) Fee structure. The trust generally provides for a reasonable fee for the trustee. A financial institution charges an annual fee based on the value of the trust property.

D. Revocable Living Trust

A revocable living trust is set up during your lifetime. You may amend or revoke the trust, as long as you are alive and competent. A revocable living trust may become irrevocable if you become incompetent, and it necessarily becomes irrevocable when you die. A living trust is sometimes called an "inter vivos" trust.

A typical living trust has two parts. The first part sets out how the trustee administers the trust while the trustor is alive. The trustee may have charge of investments or make investments as the trustor directs. The trustee also makes distributions from the trust as the trustor directs. If the trustor becomes incapacitated, the trustee then takes charge of both investments and distributions.

The second part of a living trust deals with its administration after the trustor's death. This part is a substitute for the trustor's will and directs who is to receive the trust assets. It may direct that after funeral expenses, debts, and death taxes are paid, the property be distributed and the trust terminated. Or it may direct that certain portions be kept in trust for particular beneficiaries for an additional period of time.

1. Funded Revocable Living Trust

A trust is "funded" when property is transferred to the trustee and the trustee begins managing and distributing the trust property in accordance with the trust agreement. The funded revocable living trust is discussed in the next chapter.

Establishing a funded revocable living trust involves the following three steps:

(a) Preparing and signing a trust agreement.

(b) Signing a "pour-over" will, which basically provides that if the trustor dies with any probate property, it will be transferred or "poured over" to the trust, so that the disposition of all the trustor's property will be made under the trust agreement.

(c) Transferring ownership of all of trustor's property to the trustee.

A revocable living trust which is funded when it is signed has gained popularity recently as one of the best tools for planning your estate. The major benefits and drawbacks of the funded revocable living trust are explained in the next chapter.

2. The Revocable Life Insurance Trust

The typical life insurance trust is an unfunded living trust, under which the trustor names a trustee as beneficiary of life insurance policies on the trustor's life. The trustor pays the premiums and has all rights of ownership in the policy, including the right to borrow and to change beneficiaries. The trustee has no duties (other than safekeeping the policies) until the trustor's death, at which time the trustee obtains the proceeds from the policy and administers the proceeds according to the trust agreement. The principal benefit of the revocable life insurance trust is the ability to effect distribution of the proceeds at the insured's death without probate.

E. Irrevocable Living Trusts

An irrevocable living trust, like a revocable living trust, is set up during your lifetime, but may not be amended or revoked once it is set up. You give up the right to control property placed in an irrevocable trust.

Irrevocable living trusts are used primarily to minimize income, estate, and inheritance taxes. Because you must give up control of the property you transfer, you should use irrevocable trusts only with the assistance of tax experts and only if you are satisfied that the tax benefits that you expect to receive justify the loss of control of your property.

1. Irrevocable Life Insurance Trusts

In an irrevocable life insurance trust, you either transfer cash to a trust, which purchases a life insurance policy on your life, or you transfer ownership of a policy on your life to a trustee and irrevocably relinquish all ownership. Such trusts are used as an estate and inheritance tax planning tool to exclude the proceeds from your estate at your death for estate tax purposes.

2. Charitable Remainder Trusts

Suppose you want to make a substantial gift to your favorite charity, but first want to make sure that you receive income from the gift for the rest of your life. You can do this by setting up a type of an irrevocable living trust known as the charitable remainder trust.

You can obtain income and estate tax benefits with such a trust. Suppose you have a large block of low-basis stock you want to sell. You could establish a charitable remainder trust, have the trust sell the stock and reinvest the proceeds in a mixed portfolio of securities, give you an income stream for your life, and then have the assets pass to your favorite charity at your death. You would receive the following tax benefits:

(a) You avoid the capital gain on the sale of your low-basis stock;

(b) You receive a current income tax charitable deduction for the actuarial value of the assets which the charity will receive at your death; and

(c) Your estate receives an estate tax charitable deduction for the value of the trust assets at your death.

There are two types of charitable remainder trusts. One is called an annuity trust and fixes the amount of your payments based on a percentage of the value of the assets initially transferred to the trust. The amount of the payment, once fixed, will not change for the rest of your life. For instance, if you were to transfer stock to the trust having a value of $200,000 and direct that you will receive five percent (5%) annually, you would receive $10,000 a year for the rest of your life. The other type is a unitrust and fixes the amount of your payments based on an annual revaluation of the assets. With the same example, you would receive $10,000 the first year. If at the end of the first year, the value of the portfolio had increased to $210,000, you would receive $10,500 the second year.

A charitable remainder trust can also be set up as a testamentary trust in your will or living trust. It would generate possible estate and inheritance tax savings, but no income tax savings.

F. Testamentary Trusts

A testamentary trust is set up in your will or living trust and does not go into effect or become funded until you die and the will is admitted to probate or your living trust is settled. In effect, the testator or testatrix is the trustor of a testamentary trust.

The possible uses of testamentary trusts are as varied as the needs of people setting up their estate plans. Some of the more common reasons you may want to use testamentary trusts are:

(a) to provide for your children if you die while they are minors or before they are mature enough to handle their financial affairs;

(b) to provide for a physically or mentally handicapped spouse or child or other family member. These trusts can last for the rest of the person's life;

(c) to protect children of a previous marriage. A trust for this purpose could give your spouse the income and principal to maintain his or her standard of living, and the assets of the trust could be distributed to the children after your spouse's death;

(d) to minimize the risk that part of your estate would be dissipated by a spendthrift son- or daughter-in-law;

(e) to provide financing for college education for your grandchildren;

(f) to provide support for a dependent relative;

(g) to gain income, gift, inheritance, and estate tax savings;

(h) to provide for the care of domestic or family pets, commonly known as a "pet trust."

G. Trusts and Tax Savings

As an example of a tax-savings testamentary trust, suppose you own all your property jointly with your spouse with right of survivorship, that the value of your joint estates is $2 million and that the estate tax exemption is $1 million (the exemption for 2002). If you were to die first and died in 2002, there would be no federal estate tax to pay because of your $1 million exemption. If your spouse were to die later in 2002 with an estate of $2 million, there would be federal estate and Oregon inheritance taxes to pay totaling about $460,000.

However, suppose you and your spouse were to split your assets in half, and you each set up a testamentary trust for the other in your wills or living trusts leaving instructions to the trustee to make payments to your spouse for life and at your spouse's death distribute the remaining proceeds to your children. If both deaths occurred in 2002, no tax would be paid at either your or your spouse's death. This type of trust is sometimes known as a credit shelter trust or a bypass trust. For a more detailed explanation of this trust, see chapter 16.

H.   The Duties of a Trustee

The Oregon Supreme Court describes a trustee's duty as a "grave responsibility" involving a "fundamental duty of loyalty and good faith." The principal duties involved are as follows:

(a) The duty to follow the terms of the trust agreement.

(b) The duty to exercise good faith, diligence, and prudence in investing trust property. This does not mean that the investments must always make a profit, but it does mean that the trustee should have the skills, or seek professional help, to invest wisely.

(c) The duty to protect and preserve assets.

(d) The duty to be loyal to the beneficiaries. A trustee cannot engage in any self-dealing, conflict of interest, act of fraud, or any other act of disloyalty.

(e) The duty to account for all investments. This requires keeping accurate records of all receipts and disbursements of income and principal and prohibits the trustee from commingling trust assets with the trustee's own assets.

I.   How to Select a Trustee

Because of the standards of conduct that a trustee must adhere to, the selection of a trustee itself is an important decision. If you are naming a trustee for a revocable living trust, you will normally name yourself as the initial trustee. You should name successor trustees to administer your trust in case of your incapacity and to settle your trust at your death. For an irrevocable or testamentary trust that may last for many years, you should name both the initial trustee and one or more successor trustees.

Your choice might be a relative, friend, accountant, lawyer, or trust company. A trust company is a financial institution authorized to engage in trust business and may be an independent trust company, the trust department of a full-service bank, or a trust company affiliated with a major securities firm. Certain individuals, typically former trust officers, also act as professional trustees.

Financial institutions authorized to engage in trust business with offices in Oregon are listed on the author's web site at www.rcjlaw.com.

1. Professional Management

Trust companies are in the business of trust management and have both the expertise and the experience to deal with investments and the complexities of trust administration, accounting, and taxation. An individual will probably not be able to offer you the same degree of expertise.

Whether you select an individual or a trust company, you can place some control on your investments by requiring that certain trust property not be sold, designating the types of investments that are permissible, and requiring the trustee to use an outside investment counselor.

2. Impartiality

A trusted friend or relative may be more sensitive than a trust company to the particular needs of your children or other beneficiaries. On the other hand, a trust company will be impartial at all times. Suppose, for example, that you set up a trust for your son to last until he is 25 years old. Your son may resent the implication that he cannot handle his own affairs until he is 25. The trustee has to play the bad guy role while following the terms of the trust. A trust company will have no problem being impartial, and will not likely be tempted to favor one beneficiary over another.

3. Perpetual Existence

It is unlikely that a trust company will not be around for the duration of your trust. Unlike an individual, a trust company will not become ill or incapacitated or die. A court will always appoint a successor trustee if an individual trustee dies, but then you might end up with someone as trustee you do not even know. You can minimize that risk by using a trust company. If you want to name a friend or relative, it is a good idea to name one or more alternative trustees, name co-trustees, or give adult beneficiaries the right to remove trustees and to name successor trustees.

4. Dishonesty

Unless a beneficiary files a lawsuit, a trustee is not account-able to the courts. This may tempt an individual to use trust assets for personal gain either through fraud or improper acts of self-dealing.

You can require the trustee to be bonded by a commercial surety company, but the premiums add to the cost of administering the trust and a bond is seldom used. If you feel you need to require your trustee to be bonded, then you probably need to find a different trustee.

Although trust companies are not immune from fraud and conflicts of interest, such acts are rare. In addition, trust companies are governed by regulations that minimize the risk of loss to trust beneficiaries.

5. Trustee's Fee

The fee may be the most practical consideration in choosing between a trust company and an individual. A trust company's annual fee is generally 1% to 1.5% of the value of the assets. Most trust companies have a minimum fee of $1,000 or more. This means that it usually is not cost effective to use a trust company as a trustee unless the trust property has a value of $200,000 to $250,000.

Many trust companies have fragmented fee schedules. For instance, for a living trust, many trust companies charge a one-time setup fee (typically $100 to $250), an annual fee based on a varying percentage (depending on the nature of the asset) of the value of the assets, a minimum annual fee (ranging from $1,000 to $2,500), additional transaction or hourly fees for specific services such as tax return preparation, and termination fees if you revoke the trust. Fees and fee practices vary widely among trust companies, as do investment records, experiences, and expertise in specialized areas such as management of small businesses or farms.

An individual trustee is entitled to whatever compensation you provide for in the trust agreement. Often, family members who are acting as trustees will expect only modest compensation. However, an individual may have to hire professional advisers, such as an investment adviser or an attorney, resulting in costs to the trust that are normally included in a trust company's annual fee. There may be adverse tax consequences from selecting a close family member as your trustee. Consult a tax advisor before you make your choice.

J.   Your Rights as a Beneficiary

If you are a beneficiary of a trust and believe that your trustee is not doing a good job, and you cannot resolve the problem through negotiation, you can file a lawsuit and have a court review the trustee's performance. By statute the court has the power to do the following:

(a) review the amount of compensation the trustee has paid itself and require the trustee to refund any excess amount;

(b) require the trustee to provide you with a report of all receipts and disbursements, an inventory of the trust property, and a summary of all transactions relating to the trust property, once a year; and

(c) instruct the trustee on the proper interpretation of the trust or on any matter relating to the administration, settlement, or distribution of the trust estate.

If the court finds that the trustee has been mishandling the trust it can:

(a) remove the trustee and appoint a successor;

(b) require the trustee to pay damages for any losses caused by breach of the trust; and

(c) deny or reduce the amount of the trustee's compensation.

Chapter 5

The Funded Revocable Living Trust

A. Introduction

The living trust is a popular way of avoiding probate and as a vehicle for handling your affairs in case of incapacity. It has also been touted as a way of saving taxes.

When people talk about living trusts as a way of avoiding probate, they are referring to the funded revocable living trust, which will be called a "living trust" throughout this chapter.

Do not confuse a living trust with a living will. A living will is a popular name for a document you can sign directing that you do not want tube feeding or other forms of life support if you are terminally ill. In Oregon, a living will is called an advance directive (see chapter 12).

A living trust can be the centerpiece of your estate plan. However, it has no advantage over a will or other planning tools in saving taxes, and it is not a panacea for probate avoidance. After studying living trusts, weigh the pros and cons carefully (see section I) before deciding whether it is right for you.

B. The Trust Documents

Establishing a living trust involves two major steps: signing the trust agreement and related documents, and funding the trust by retitling assets into the name of the trustee. The basic documents are the trust agreement, a pour-over will, and one or more financial powers of attorney. In order to complete your estate plan, you should also consider signing an advance directive, an anatomical gift card, and letters of instructions which may cover funeral and burial instructions.

A basic living trust agreement has two main parts. The first part directs how the trustee administers the trust during your lifetime. The trustee invests and manages the trust assets and makes distributions from the trust according to your directions so long as you are capable of giving directions. If you become incapacitated, the trustee then takes charge of both investments and distributions.

If you are able to handle your financial affairs yourself, then name yourself as the initial trustee and manage the trust. A successor trustee, named in the trust agreement, steps in and takes charge of your financial affairs if you become incapacitated, or if you ask the successor trustee to take charge.

If you are the acting trustee at your death, then your successor trustee steps in and settles your trust. If you need help with your financial affairs at the time you set up the trust, then you name someone other than yourself, such as a family member or trust company, as the initial trustee, who then will settle your trust at your death.

The second part of the basic living trust directs how your trust will be administered after your death. It contains the "dispositive provisions" (provisions that direct how your property will be distributed at your death) which would normally be in your will if you did not have a living trust. It may direct that after all your funeral bills, claims, expenses, and taxes are paid, your trustee is to distribute your trust estate to family members and then terminate the trust. Or it may direct that certain portions be kept in one or more testamentary trusts for particular beneficiaries for an additional period of time after your death.

Although one of the primary benefits of a living trust is probate avoidance, you still need a will, in case probate property gets overlooked or is intentionally kept in probate ownership and is not transferred to your trust during your lifetime.

There may be other reasons which may make it necessary to probate your estate; for instance, to make certain tax elections that only a personal representative can make, or to cut off creditors' claims. In the will, you name personal representatives, and you direct that if you die with any probate property, your personal representative is to transfer it or "pour" it over to the trustee of your living trust. This is the reason for the name, "pour-over" will. The pour-over will helps assure that all your probate and trust assets will be distributed under a coordinated plan.

The third major document you sign is a financial power of attorney. Normally you name each trustee, including each successor trustee, as agent under the power of attorney. The two primary purposes of this document are to enable an agent to transfer assets to your trust if you become incapacitated and to handle financial matters (such as filing your income tax returns) that cannot be handled by your trustee.

C. Living Trusts for Married Couples

Married couples considering living trusts have several options. They can do a joint trust, or they can each have a separate trust. A trust is considered a joint trust if it has two trustors, regardless of the number of trustees.

1. The Joint and Survivorship Living Trust

The joint and survivorship trust is typically used by a married couple whose combined net worth is less than the estate tax exemption ($1 million in 2002) and is not likely to reach that amount, and who own most of their property jointly with right of survivorship. Both spouses are typically the initial trustees. If one spouse dies or becomes incapacitated, the other spouse continues to act as sole trustee. After the incapacity or death of the first spouse, the other spouse has full legal control over the trust and may revoke or amend it. At the surviving spouse's death, their trust estate can be settled without probate.

2. The Common Joint Living Trust

This joint trust is used by married couples whose net worth exceeds the estate tax exemption ($1 million in 2002) and who plan to include provisions in their trust to minimize death taxes. It can also be used by couples who have children by prior marriages. It is basically two trusts in one, with each spouse's trust owning 100%

of that spouse's separate property and 50% of all property owned jointly by the couple. The two trusts own the couple's joint property as tenants in common.

Upon the death of the first spouse, the joint trust is divided into two basic trusts. The first is a family trust, which consists of the deceased spouse's separate property and the deceased spouse's half interest in the joint property. The second is a survivor's trust, containing the remaining assets. The family trust may be divided into additional subtrusts for tax-planning purposes.

3. The Community Property Joint Living Trust

This trust is designed for married couples who move to Oregon from a community property state. There are certain tax advantages to community property, which can be preserved by use of this trust, even though a couple moves to Oregon, which is not a community property state. This trust operates similarly to the common joint living trust, except that the joint property of the couple is owned by the trustees as community property rather than as tenants in common.

4. Separate Trusts for Each Spouse

Each spouse can have a separate basic living trust. Married couples in second marriages and married couples who plan to do tax planning trusts, but prefer to separate their joint assets rather than have a common joint living trust, are the best candidates for separate trusts.

D. Funding the Trust

The second major step in establishing a living trust is to "fund" it by retitling your property into the name of the trustee. If your primary goal is to avoid probate at your death, all your property must be in your trust or in other forms of nonprobate ownership at your death. However, it may be inadvisable, impractical, or impossible to transfer all your property to your trust.

1. General Funding Rules

The following are some general funding rules:

(a) Each separate asset must be retitled. You cannot do a blanket transfer of all assets in a single document.

(b) Each asset must be listed in the name of the trustee rather than the trust. It is a peculiarity of trust law that a trust cannot own property. Title should be some version or abbreviation of this: "John Doe, or his successor in trust, as trustee of the John Doe Living Trust dated July 1, 200-."

(c) For some types of property, such as a life insurance policy or annuity, you list the trustee as beneficiary rather than owner.

(d) Oregon's small estate law permits transfer of probate property through the inexpensive use of a small estate affidavit if the value of the property is under certain thresholds (see chapter 15). You can thus keep some assets, such as a motor vehicle or a checking account, out of your trust.

(e) Certain tax-sensitive assets should not be transferred to a trust without the advice of a tax expert. Examples are tax-deferred annuities, individual retirement accounts (IRAs), stock in a closely-held corporation, incentive stock options, and rental real property with passive activity losses.

(f) When you retitle assets, financial institutions and title companies require information about your trust. Some financial institutions require you to complete a special form containing basic information about the trust, such as the date of the trust and the names of the acting and successor trustees. Others require you to provide them with a complete copy of your trust agreement.

One of the attractions of a living trust is that it can help you preserve the privacy of your financial affairs. In order to preserve your privacy, you should check to see if the financial institution will accept a certification of trust (see Sample #1). A financial institution relying on the form is relieved from liability to any person. If a certification of trust is not acceptable, provide excerpts from your trust agreement, such as the first and last pages and the pages containing the trustees' powers. Try not to disclose the dispositive provisions of your trust, that is, the provisions that direct how your property will be distributed at your death.

Once you have completed the funding of your trust, you should prepare a schedule, commonly known as Schedule A, listing all the assets in the trust. This will help you keep track of the assets in the trust and will assist your successor trustee in identifying the assets which are in the trust. Preparing and signing the schedule to your trust does not excuse you from transferring assets to the trust. You should update the schedule periodically.

Sample #1
Certification of Trust

I, _____John Smith_____, trustee of the _John Smith_ Living Trust dated _May 3 , 200-_ make this certification pursuant to Oregon law.

1. **Trust.** The trust is presently in existence. It was executed on _May 3 , 200-_.

2. **Trustor and Trustee.** I am the trustor and am currently the sole trustee of the trust.

3. **Trust Powers.** Under the terms of the trust agreement, the trustee is given powers granted a trustee under the Uniform Trustee's Powers Act set forth in ORS 128.003 - 128.045, including the right to sell, exchange, assign, lease, encumber, or otherwise alienate all or any part of the trust estate on such terms as the trustee shall determine.

4. **Trustee's Mailing Address.** My mailing address as current acting trustee is: _555 SW Zero Street, Portland, Oregon 97200_

5. **Trust Revocable.** The trust is revocable. Only the trustor can revoke the trust.

6. **Modification of Trust.** The trust can be modified, amended, or revoked by the trustor only.

7. **One Trustee Only.** I am acting alone as trustee and have authority to exercise trust powers alone.

8. **Taxpayer Identification Number.** The trust taxpayer identification number is _____.

9. **Title To Trust Property**. Trust property is to be titled as follows: <u>John Smith</u>, or <u>his</u> successor in trust, as trustee of the <u>John Smith</u> Living Trust dated <u>May 3</u>, 200.-, as amended.

10.**No Change In Trust.** The trust has not been revoked, modified, or amended in any manner that would cause the representations contained in this certification to be incorrect.

DATED: June 1   , 200-.   <u>John Smith</u>
                                                        Trustee

STATE OF OREGON   )
) ss.
County of Multnomah)

This instrument was acknowledged before me on <u>June 1</u>, 200-, by <u>John Smith</u> as acting trustee.

                              _____
                              NOTARY PUBLIC FOR OREGON
                              My Commission Expires:

2. Real Property

You transfer title to your family home, recreational home, and other real property to your trust by signing a deed and recording it in the county where the property is located. Generally you should use the same form of deed, typically a warranty deed, that was used when you acquired the property. The trustee should be listed as an additional insured party on your fire and liability insurance policies. The "insured" is the person who is protected by an insurance policy.

If you have a loan secured by a mortgage or trust deed on the property, obtain your lender's consent to transfer the property to your trust. Mortgages and trust deeds commonly have a "due-on-transfer" clause which gives the lender the right to call the loan and declare you in default if you transfer title to the property without consent. If you transfer rental real property to your trust, also assign each lease or rental agreement to the trustee.

If you own a mortgage or trust deed, typically because you have loaned money or sold property, or if you have sold real property on contract, you can transfer your interest in these assets to your trustee. If you are receiving payments through a collection escrow, then you may need to assign the collection agreement to your trustee and deposit new deeds or similar documents in escrow. A collection escrow is a three-way contract between an escrow company and the buyer and seller. The buyer makes payments to the escrow company, who in turn sends the payments to the seller. The escrow company provides both parties with annual reports of all payments.

3. Other Assets

If you own stocks and bonds from many different companies and hold all the certificates, you will simplify transfer of your securities to your trustee if you deposit all your securities in a brokerage account in the name of the trustee.

Transfer untitled property, such as your furniture, jewelry, and other tangible personal property, by a bill of sale or assignment.

E. Tax Aspects of Living Trusts

In most aspects, living trusts are tax-neutral. A living trust will neither save you taxes nor cost you extra taxes.

1. Income Taxes

During your lifetime, you are treated as owner of all assets in your trust for income tax purposes. Your trust is considered a "grantor" trust, which means that all income earned on trust assets is deemed earned by you and is reported by you on your individual income tax returns.

If you are your own trustee, then when you transfer assets to your trust, you continue to use your own Social Security Number as your taxpayer identification number. You do not need to file a separate income tax return for the trust.

If you are not your own trustee, then the trustee can use your Social Security Number as the taxpayer identification number for the trust, provided you give the trustee a completed IRS form, known as a W-9, verifying your Social Security

Number. The trustee must give you an annual statement of income and expenses, but is not required to file income tax returns for the trust.

At your death, your trust becomes an irrevocable trust and ceases to be a grantor trust. Your trustee must file annual trust income tax returns and your trust must pay tax on any income that is not distributed to your beneficiaries during the year the trust receives the income. These returns are similar to the income tax returns which a personal representative would have to file if your estate required probate. These returns are called fiduciary income tax returns. Normally a trust can be settled and distribution completed within a year, which means that only one set of income tax returns must be filed for the trust.

2. Gift Taxes

Because you have a right to revoke your trust, you do not make a gift for federal gift tax purposes when you transfer assets to the trust.

If you plan to make annual exclusion gifts ($11,000 in 2002), your trustee, upon instructions from you, may make gifts directly to your intended recipients. (The amount of annual exclusion gifts is indexed for inflation and increased to $11,000 from $10,000 in 2002). If you have established an annual gift-giving program and would want your trustee to continue it in case of your incapacity, insert express language in your trust and your power of attorney authorizing both your trustee and your agent to make such gifts if you cannot.

3. Death Taxes

Placing assets in a living trust does not save you any federal estate or Oregon inheritance taxes. Because of your right to revoke your trust up to the moment of your death, all assets in your trust at your death are considered part of your gross estate subject to death taxation.

Many promoters of living trusts tout the death tax savings which you can obtain from a living trust. Typically they are talking about the so-called bypass or credit shelter trusts used by married couples and described in chapter 16. Such trusts can be set up in either a will or a living trust, and setting them up in a living trust is neither better nor worse than setting them up in your will.

F.   Periodic Review

If you establish a living trust, then periodic review, perhaps once a year, is essential to assure that you achieve the benefits of the living trust. A good time to review your living trust is at income tax time, when you have year-end statements of your investments and can easily prepare a net worth statement. The purpose of the review is to assure that your living trust reflects your current wishes and goals and that all or substantially all your assets are in your trust or in other nonprobate forms of ownership. Review your trust agreement and related documents as well as the title documents to all your assets. Such a review can also alert you to the possibility that your estate may have grown to the point that you need to worry about estate taxes, or conversely, that changes in the estate tax laws may now make it unnecessary to do estate tax planning.

Periodic review is more essential with a living trust than with a will. If you purchase or inherit assets after you establish a living trust, then make sure that your new assets are in your trustee's name and not in your name individually. If you leave new assets in your individual name, then they will be probate assets requiring a probate of your estate at your death.

Review, and if necessary, revise your trust agreement because of changes in your circumstances. One example is your marriage, remarriage, divorce, or annulment. Your marriage or remarriage automatically revokes your will, and the dissolution or annulment of your marriage automatically revokes any provision in your will for your former spouse. This is not true, however, with a living trust. A marriage or divorce does not automatically revoke or amend your living trust unless you so provide in your living trust.

G.   Settlement at Trustor's Death

A primary benefit of a living trust is the avoidance of probate at your death. However, having a living trust, fully funded, to avoid a probate at your death, does not necessarily mean that there will be no delay or costs in settling your affairs.

Your trustee must follow many of the same steps that a personal representative must follow if your estate required probate. The primary differences are that your trustee can settle your trust without court supervision, without filing an inventory or accounting with the court, without the formal notices to creditors and to heirs, and without regard to the various probate waiting periods and deadlines. This gives your trustee more flexibility than a personal representative has in scheduling distributions.

Your trustee's primary duties are: to collect, take control of, and manage all assets, and preserve and protect assets; to pay all debts and claims against the trust; to pay all income, gift, and death taxes; and to distribute the assets in accordance with the trust agreement.

These steps cannot be accomplished within a day, a week, or even a month. A simple trust can probably be settled within 60 to 90 days after the trustor's death. A typical settlement period is three to six months. If your estate is large enough to require the filing of death tax returns, settlement may take a year or longer.

There will also be costs incurred in settling your trust. Your trustee will probably need the assistance of an attorney, but attorney fees should be lower than if your estate required a probate. Your trustee may also need a tax advisor, one or more appraisers, and other professional advisors.

H. Creditors' Claims

Creditors can reach assets in your trust for up to two years after your death and possibly even longer. Unlike a probate (See chapter 14), your trustee is not required to give notice of your death to creditors. However, if your trustee is aware of or concerned about the possibility of such claims, your trustee can follow an optional procedure to notify creditors that you have died. By following this procedure, your trustee can shorten the period of time during which creditors can assert claims to four months after required notices are given. After the expiration of the four-month period, your trustee can make distribution without concern about unknown or disputed claims.

The trustee commences the procedure by filing a petition with the probate court to determine claims of creditors. After the petition is filed, the trustee causes a notice to creditors to be published in a local newspaper, makes a search for creditors and gives notice to known creditors. A claim is barred unless the creditor submits the claim to the trustee within four months after the first publication of the public notice or, for known creditors to whom the trustee gives notice, within four months after such notice, whichever is longer.

If no claims are filed within the four-month period, then the trustee files a petition to close, and the probate court enters an order closing the proceeding. If a creditor submits a claim which the trustee disputes, then the probate court determines the validity of the claim, after which the proceeding is closed.

This streamlined procedure can remove uncertainty about creditors' claims without forcing the trustee to follow all the steps of a formal probate. The trustee is not required to file the pour-over will, the trust agreement, an inventory of assets or any accountings with the court, so the contents of the will and trust and the nature and extent of your estate do not become a matter of public record.

I.   The Pros and Cons

This section outlines some of the major benefits and drawbacks of the revocable living trust. The advantages include the following:

(a) A living trust is an effective tool for handling your financial affairs if you are incapacitated. In the trust agreement, you can direct who will handle your affairs by naming a co-trustee or successor trustee. You can also state how incapacity will be determined and how your affairs will be handled.

Generally, a trust is more dependable than a power of attorney, which may not be accepted by banks, insurance companies, stockbrokers, or title companies. A trust is also generally preferable to a court-supervised conservatorship, which is expensive and cumbersome and makes the facts of your incapacity and the nature and extent of your financial affairs matters of public record.

(b) A living trust can avoid the delay and expense of probate. A trust will survive you, and on your death there is no need to probate property in your trust because the legal ownership of assets in the trust is with the trustee.

(c) Probate is a court proceeding open to the public. A living trust is a private arrangement and your financial affairs are not subject to public scrutiny at your death.

(d) If you have real property in more than one state, a living trust will save you the expense of multiple probates.

(e) A living trust is a flexible estate planning tool. You can create a self-administered living trust where you name yourself as trustee and beneficiary. With this type of trust, you continue to manage and direct your investment portfolio as you do now. You have full discretion over how to invest your assets and how to use the income from those assets. You have the additional protection of naming a successor trustee to take over the management of your trust if you die or become incapacitated. If you prefer to have help with your investments, you can select and name a professional manager, such as a bank or investment advisor, as your trustee.

(f) A living trust can help assure a coordinated disposition of all your property. When you rely primarily on a will, it is easy to forget that many of your assets, such as life insurance and retirement benefits, may not go through probate and to overlook the need to coordinate the disposition of your probate and non-probate property.

Some of the disadvantages include the following:

(a) A living trust is more expensive and time consuming to set up than a will, and is a more complicated document than a will. Attorney fees for preparation of a living trust will be higher than for preparation of a will. You may have recording and other transfer fees. If you use a trust company as trustee, you will have annual trustee's fees to pay.

(b) In addition to preparing and executing the trust agreement, you must also transfer ownership of all assets into the name of the trustee. This forces you to organize, review, and redo title documents and beneficiary designations to all the property you wish to put into trust. It has been likened to probating your own estate while you are still alive.

(c) Once the trust is in place, you must regularly monitor your affairs to assure that all your property is in the name of the trustee. In addition, if you are acting as your own trustee, you may find it more difficult to deal with stock transfer agents, life insurance companies, and title insurance companies.

(d) Unlike a probate, with a living trust the time frame within which creditors' claims may be filed is not shortened so as to bar claims after your death.

(e) During probate, a court supervises your personal representative. If he or she misbehaves, your beneficiaries can voice their objections. The personal representative must file accountings with the court, and probate records are subject to public scrutiny, which encourages honest, punctual, and responsible administration of probate estates.

There are no such built-in incentives for a trustee settling a living trust at your death. The trustee proceeds to settle your trust (or fail to settle it) without court supervision or public scrutiny and beneficiaries only know whatever the trustee tells them. A trustee must provide accountings to beneficiaries only if they request accountings. If a trustee mismanages your trust after your death and does not voluntarily provide your benefici- aries with accountings, the beneficiaries must file a lawsuit against the trustee to obtain accountings and try to correct the trustee's misdeeds. There are few areas of trusts where you have to trust your trustee more, in the literal meaning of the word, than in your selection of the trustee of your living trust.

(f) There are no significant tax benefits or drawbacks with a revocable living trust. For income, gift, and estate tax purposes, you are still treated as the owner of all the property in your trust. Contrary to what some trust promoters claim, a living trust is no better or worse than a will as a planning tool for minimizing or eliminating death taxes.

In summary, you are probably a good candidate for a living trust if you are at or beyond retirement age and are more concerned about preserving and managing your estate than building it, or if you have become concerned about your own capacity to manage your financial affairs. You also must be committed to spend the time and money to establish, fund and maintain a living trust.

Chapter 6

What Happens When You Die Without a Will?

A. Introduction

This chapter might well be subtitled "The Costs of Neglect" because of the frequently unexpected consequences and the unnecessary costs that can result when someone dies with probate property and without a will.

One of the risks is the possibility of distribution of your probate property to your "laughing heirs," that is, distant relatives you never met or knew. Another risk is the possibility of extra costs in settling your estate. These extra costs are built into a probate system in part to protect your heirs from your own lack of planning.

This chapter deals only with what happens to your probate property when you die without a will. Your nonprobate property will not go to your heirs; it will go to those persons who are the designated recipients based on the form of nonprobate property. For example, suppose you die without a will. You leave a house and a savings account in your own name, some life insurance with a named beneficiary, and some securities owned jointly with right of survivorship with another person. Your house and savings account will go through probate to your heirs, but your life insurance proceeds and securities will not. They will go to the named beneficiary and the other joint owner.

B.   Who Are Your Heirs?

If you die without a will, your heirs are determined by Oregon's laws of intestate succession, which are sometimes called the laws of descent and distribution. The purpose of these laws is to approximate the desires of the person who dies intestate, that is, the person who dies with probate property and without a will. However, no law can anticipate every individual's specific desires. If you want all your wishes to be met, you should have a will.

To be your heir under the laws of intestate succession, a person must either be your spouse or must be related to you by blood or adoption. This means that none of your probate property will go to close friends, a favorite charity, or to relatives by marriage like a son-in-law or stepchildren. This is one of the costs of neglect.

1. Heirs and Devisees

The term "heir" refers solely to a relative who is entitled under law to a share of your probate property when you die without a will. This term should not be confused with the word "devisee," which refers to any person or organization that is entitled to a share of your probate property under the terms of your will.

2. Surviving Spouse

The term "surviving spouse" refers to the person to whom the decedent was legally married at the decedent's death. To be considered legally married, a couple residing in Oregon must have their marriage solemnized. Oregon requires a ceremonial marriage and does not recognize common-law marriage, unless it was consummated in a state that recognizes common-law marriages (see chapter 10). A couple is considered to be legally married to each other if one spouse dies while a marriage dissolution is pending and did not become final before the spouse's death.

3. Issue and Lineal Descendants

A lineal descendant is any living child, grandchild, great-grandchild, or any later generation in the same line of descent. The term "issue" has more limited meaning. It refers to any living lineal descendant except a lineal descendant of another living lineal descendant.

Only lineal descendants who are issue can inherit from you. For example, suppose you had two children, Bob and Ron. Bob has one child, Aaron, and Ron has one child, Susan. Bob dies before you do so at your death you have three lineal descendants: Ron, Aaron, and Susan. But only Ron and Aaron are your issue. Susan is not because she is the lineal descendant of a living lineal descendant, that is, Ron's daughter. Susan would not inherit from you.

4. Representation

Representation refers to the method of determining each heir's shares when they are of unequal kinship. Suppose that you die without a surviving spouse and are survived by your daughter, Mary, and by the two children of a deceased daughter, Ruth. Mary would receive 50% of your probate property. Ruth's two children would split her 50% share, each receiving 25% of your probate property. Ruth's two children receive their share "by representation."

If your heirs are of equal kinship, they share your probate property equally. If, in the example above, both your daughters died before you, all your grandchildren would share equally in your probate property.

C. Who Gets What?

If you die without a will and with probate property, your heirs and their share of probate property are determined as follows:

(a) If you are survived by your spouse but no children or other issue, or if all your children or other issue are also issue of your spouse, as in the typical first marriage, your spouse receives all your probate property.

(b) If you are survived by a spouse and children or other issue, and if one or more of your issue are not issue of your spouse, as might occur in a second marriage, your spouse receives 50% of your probate property and your issue share the remaining 50%.

(c) If you are survived by children or other issue, but no spouse, your issue share all the property.

(d) If you die without a surviving spouse or issue, then your parents are your heirs. If both parents are alive and married to each other at the time of your death, they will receive your real property as tenants by the entirety and your personal property as joint tenants with right of survivorship. If they are not married to each other, they receive all your property as tenants in common. If you are survived by only one parent, that parent receives all your probate property.

(e) If you die without any spouse, issue, or parents, your brothers or sisters (your siblings) will be your heirs. A deceased sibling's issue (i.e., your nephews and nieces) will receive that sibling's share by representation.

(f) If you have no heirs in the above categories, then your grandparents are next in line. If all four grandparents are alive, each of them would receive 25% of your probate property. If either set of grandparents are married to each other, they receive their share jointly with right of survivorship. The rule of representation applies to your grandparents' issue so that uncles and aunts and their children (your cousins) become your heirs if either set of your grandparents die before you do.

(g) If you have no relatives in the above categories, the state of Oregon becomes your sole heir. This is known as "escheat." All your probate property will be distributed to the Oregon Division of State Lands.

    With no will, there is a risk that your estate may be distributed to "laughing heirs" at your death, that is, distant relatives whom you never knew during your lifetime and who laugh all the way to the bank with the inheritance they receive from you. In one estate handled by the author, a man died without a will and without a surviving wife, children or siblings. His closest relatives were various first cousins. He had fifteen first cousins, some of whom were deceased. Parts of his estate went to first cousins thrice removed, that is, great-grandchildren of deceased first cousins, some of whom received a 1/270th share of the estate. There were over 35 heirs, most of whom did not know the decedent and never heard of him until after his death.

If you own probate real property in more than one state, and you die without a will, your estate settlement will be more complicated. Your heirs will be determined by the laws of intestate succession of the state where the real property is located. Although most state laws are similar to Oregon's law, they are not always the same.

D. Special Rules Governing Heirs

1. Afterborn Heirs

An heir conceived before your death and born after your death inherits as though he or she were alive at your death.

2. Survivorship by 120 Hours

If an heir dies within 120 hours after you die, he or she is considered to have predeceased you. This rule may make the probate of an heir's estate unnecessary, where that heir dies a short time after the deceased.

3. Persons of Half Blood

Persons of half blood inherit the same share they would inherit if they were of full blood. For instance, if you had been married twice and have a daughter by each marriage, your daughters are half-sisters to each other. However, both would be considered your heirs and heirs of each other.

4. Adopted Children

Generally, under Oregon law, an adopted person is treated as a birth child of the adoptive parents for all purposes of intestate succession, and ceases to be treated as a child of the birth parents. This means that if you are adopted, your issue are all treated as if you were the birth child of your adoptive parents. Similarly, your adoptive parents and their issue or other heirs are treated as if your adopted parents were your birth parents.

For example, suppose an adopted child were to die without spouse or issue after his or her adoptive parents had died, and that the adoptive parents had birth children of their own. The birth children would be entitled to inherit from the adopted child as if that child had been a birth brother or sister.

There are two exceptions to the general rule that an adopted person ceases to be the child of both birth parents.

(a) If you have a child and you then marry or remarry, and the child is adopted by your new spouse, the other birth parent of your child would no longer be considered a birth parent, although you would.

Take the situation of a divorce where the mother is granted custody of a minor child and the father has no interest in the child. The mother remarries and the new husband wants to adopt the minor child to seal the new family relationship. The birth father, desiring to be relieved of his child support obligation, consents, and the parent-child relationship between the birth father and the child is terminated. If the natural father later dies without a will, the child would not inherit from him, but the child would inherit from the birth mother if she died without a will.

(b) If a birth parent dies, the other birth parent remarries, and the child is adopted by the new spouse, the adopted child continues to be considered a child of the deceased birth parent; in effect, the child is considered as having three parents for purposes of intestate succession.

For example, say a birth mother dies, the father remarries, and the new wife adopts the child. Then the birth mother's mother, who would be the child's birth grandmother, dies without a will. The child would be considered an issue of his grandmother for purposes of intestate succession and would take all or part of the birth mother's share of the grandmother's estate by representation.

5. Unmarried Parents

In Oregon, a child born out of wedlock has the same rights of inheritance as a birth child. The only requirement is that the father's paternity of the child born out of wedlock must be established during the child's life, either by appropriate legal procedures, or by the father's written acknowledgment.

E. Other Costs of Neglect

Besides not being able to choose your own heirs, you will create other problems if you die without a will. For example, the probate court will select the personal representative for your estate. When there is no will, this person is known as the administrator (or administratrix, if female). The court gives preference in the following order for the appointment:

(a) Your surviving spouse, or a person selected by your spouse;

(b) Your nearest relative or a person selected by your nearest relative;

(c) Certain government officials; and

(d) Any other person.

The personal representative must file a surety bond to protect the heirs and creditors from any breach of duty. A commercial surety bond will cost about $5 per $1,000 of value of probate property, and must be renewed annually. In a will, the testator typically waives the bond requirement to save this expense.

If an heir is a minor, the court will require that a conservatorship be established to protect the inheritance unless it is small enough to distribute to some responsible adult or financial institution. If a conservatorship is required, you will not have any say in the appointment of a conservator. A surviving parent is not permitted to use the minor's inheritance to support the child.

If you die leaving a minor child and the other parent is deceased, the court must appoint a guardian. If you have no will (or other documents) listing your choice of guardian, the court may appoint a relative whom you would think totally unfit to care for your child.

You also reduce the risk of arguments among heirs by having a will. Suppose, for example, that you had three parcels of probate real property and three heirs entitled to equal shares. The heirs could agree to take one parcel each, but if they cannot agree, the personal representative would have to sell the three parcels and split the proceeds. If you have a will, you can direct who receives what property and thus minimize the risk that valuable family property will be sold.

Chapter 7

All About Wills

This chapter focuses on the mechanics of making a will. Who can make a will? What are the requirements of a valid will? How is a will revoked?

A. What the Words Mean

There are several important terms necessary to an understanding of a discussion of wills.

(a) The person making the will is called a *testator* if male, a *testatrix* if female.

(b) A *personal representative* is the person or financial institution you name in your will to settle your probate estate. This person is also called an *executor (executrix* if female).

(c) A *codicil* is an amendment to a will. A codicil must meet the same requirements for validity as the will.

(d) To *devise* (verb) means to give or dispose of property under a will. A *devise* (noun) is a gift or disposition of property under a will.

(e) A *devisee* is a person entitled to receive property under a will. This person may also be called a beneficiary, recipient, or distributee.

At one time Oregon law made a distinction between gifts of real property and gifts of personal property under a will. A *bequest* was a gift of personal property and a *devise* was a gift of real property. To *bequeath* meant to make a gift of personal property under a will. Current Oregon law makes no distinction between gifts of real and personal property. A *devise* refers to gifts of any property under a will, real or personal.

B.   What Is a Will?

A will is a document in which you direct who will receive your probate property at your death and who will be in charge of settling your estate.

A will is unique among legal documents because it has no legal effect until you die. This unique feature of wills has several aspects:

(a) You can amend or revoke your will at any time prior to your death, provided you have the mental capacity to do so. Even if you have made a contract not to change your will, that contract will not bar you from changing or revoking your will, but it may subject you or your estate to damages for breach of contract.

(b) A will does not affect your right and control of your probate property. You continue to be free to buy, sell, give away, consume, mortgage, or otherwise deal with your property without restriction. Even if you leave specific property to a specific person, you are not restricted from selling the property or even giving it to someone else while you are alive.

(c) Conversely, no person to whom you leave property in your will has any legal claim to the property until you die. As long as you are alive, your devisees have only an expectancy, which may or may not ripen into a legal claim. You may change your will, outlive the devisee, or sell or give away the property. This is why it may not be wise to tell people that you are leaving property to them in your will.

(d) A will determines the distribution of probate property that you own at death. Therefore, a will must take into account the possible events that may occur between the date you make the will and the date of your death.

C.   What Makes a Will Valid?

To make a valid will, you must meet these four requirements:

(a) You must be over the age of majority.

(b) You must have the mental capacity to make a will.

(c) The will must be the product of your own mind and not of someone else's, whether because of improper or undue influence, duress, or fraud.

(d) You must follow the required formalities.

You must meet the same requirements to make a valid amendment or codicil to your will and to revoke your will.

1. Age Requirement

To make a valid will, you must be 18 years of age or older or be lawfully married. A 17-year-old can marry. Thus, a 17-year-old married person can make a will.

2. Mental Capacity

The second requirement is that you be of sound mind or that you have what is known as "testamentary capacity." To have testamentary capacity you must meet the following conditions:

(a) You understand that you are signing a document declaring the manner in which you want to dispose of your property at your death.

(b) You must know the nature and extent of your property. You do not need to know the exact size of your estate, but you must have a genuine knowledge as to its nature and extent.

(c) You must know, without prompting, who your heirs are (i.e., those persons who would be entitled to inherit from you if you did not have a will). This is discussed in chapter 6. Your heirs are also known as your "next-of-kin" or the "natural objects of your bounty."

(d) You must make rational disposition of your property.

You must have testamentary capacity at the moment you sign your will. Whether or not you have such capacity before or afterwards is not controlling. You do not need the same level of mental capacity to make a will as you do to convey property or enter contracts. Thus, you can have testamentary capacity even though you are developmentally disabled, have a mental or severe physical illness, are on your death bed, are under a guardianship or conservatorship, make an eccentric disposition of your property or have eccentric living habits, are vision or hearing impaired or illiterate, or do not speak or write English. In each case, it depends on whether or not you meet the four requirements at the moment you make your will.

Here are some examples from Oregon court decisions where persons were found to have testamentary capacity in spite of serious mental or physical problems.

a. Developmental disability

In his childhood, Alvin had an illness diagnosed as "brain fever," which retarded his mental development. He spent nine years in the first grade and never learned to read and write, but his mother did teach him to sign his name. He was slow in conversation and slow to understand. Nevertheless, he was generally self-sufficient and knew all about his property and how to protect his interest in it. When he made a will leaving everything to his friends and excluding his heirs, the court found that he had testamentary capacity and upheld the will.

b. Mental illness

Aletha was found to have testamentary capacity even though she had been mentally ill both before and after she signed her will. After she signed her will in her attorney's office, she was taken into custody by the police and confined until she was committed to the state hospital the next day. Her illness on occasion took the form of auditory hallucinations, such as hearing voices, and she had a persecution complex which was described as a schizophrenic reaction.

Joan was 84 years old when she signed her will. She had chronic bronchitis, arteriosclerosis, influenza, a bad cough, and was delirious and weak. She heard voices, believed in the presence of a man in her house who was not there, and she frequently heard cats on her roof, although none were there. She also was found to have testamentary capacity.

c. Extreme physical illness

Randi signed her will when she was 85 years old, the day after she suffered acute congestive heart failure. Four days later she died. James signed his will the day before he died. Both wills were found valid.

d. Eccentric living, behavior, and disposition

Frank was described as an oddball. He became increasingly slovenly shortly before his death and his eating habits and person were incredibly filthy. He failed to care for and often did not feed his livestock, and dead animals rotted about his farm. He took care of nothing and lived on four dozen eggs a week, which he cooked in a pressure cooker. He slept in his clothes and wore rain gear and rubber boots continuously. In his will he ignored his sister and gave $1 to a brother who died a month before the will was signed. In spite of all this, the court held that Frank had testamentary capacity.

3. Undue Influence

The next requirement for a valid will is that it be the product of your own mind and not of someone else's. A will resulting from fraud, duress, or the strong influence of some other person is considered the product of someone else's mind.

For instance, a will can be the result of fraudulent conduct by a beneficiary, either dealing with the signing of the will directly, such as misrepresenting its contents, or misrepresenting the facts on which the will is based.

For example, Alise was in her eighties in 1947, weighed about 285 pounds, was strongwilled, had a good mind, and expected absolute honesty from those dealing with her, believing, according to the court, the old adage that a person's word is his or her bond. When a promise was made to her, she expected and demanded that it be kept as given. She was particularly fond of one of her cousins, Margot, who lived in Illinois. Alise had an agreement with Margot that should Alise ever become seriously ill, Margot would come to her. Alise became ill in July, and Margot came out and stayed with her until August 14, when Alise signed a will leaving the bulk of her estate to her cousins, including Margot.

In September, Alise became seriously ill again and went to bed and never got up. At this point, Clara, who was the wife of Alise's stepson, entered the picture. Alise directed Clara to write Margot and have her come out because of Alise's illness. Clara, however, did not write, although Margot regularly wrote to Alise. Because of Clara's refusal to communicate with Margot, Alise developed a growing distrust and loss of confidence in Margot because she did not keep her promise to come when Alise got sick. As a result, in December 1947, Alise changed her will, leaving only $1,000 to Margot and her cousin, and the residue of her estate to Clara and others. The court concluded that Alise was the victim of Clara's deception, that it was Clara's failure to inform Margot that she should come and her failure to communicate Margot's letters to Alise that caused Alise to substantially disinherit Margot. The December 1947 will was declared invalid as a result of Clara's conduct.

A will is also invalid if a person influencing the will by his or her conduct gets an unfair advantage by devices which reasonable people would consider improper. This does not prevent advice-giving or kindnesses or confidential relationships between you and a beneficiary. However, if a beneficiary under a will obtains his or her share by means of an unfair advantage, subterfuge, misrepresentation, or other conduct, the will will be set aside.

For instance, in 1971, Sophia signed a will naming one of her two daughters as her sole beneficiary. Shortly thereafter she hired a certain Wayne to manage her farm. He had come to Oregon with a criminal record, so assumed a new name. From June 1972 until Sophia's death in November 1973, Sophia and Wayne both occupied the house on the farm. At the time, Sophia was 77 years old, in poor health, and suffering from various physical disabilities, but apparently mentally sharp and strongwilled. Eventually, Sophia signed a new will naming Wayne as sole beneficiary. The court held that Wayne had exercised undue influence over Sophia, and held the new will invalid. The new will was prepared by a friend of Wayne's, who had also come from California and had a criminal record too. The court found the following factors present, which indicated improper influence by Wayne.

a. Procurement

Wayne, as beneficiary, participated in the preparation of the will by providing his friend with the description of the farm, arranging for his friend to type the will, and also arranging for the witnesses to the will.

b. Lack of independent advice

Sophia did not have any independent advice from her own attorney or other persons.

c. Secrecy and haste

Apparently one reason why no lawyer was engaged to prepare the will, according to the court, was Wayne's desire to keep it a secret. There was also evidence that there was considerable haste in the preparation of the will, which was signed four days before Sophia's death.

d. Change in attitude toward others

It was significant to the court that Sophia was disinheriting one of her daughters, obviously reflecting displeasure with her, which the court felt was probably caused by Wayne.

e. Unnatural gift

It is possible to make an eccentric gift. However, an eccentric gift will be weighed in determining whether undue influences existed. In this case, when coupled with other facts, undue influence was indicated. It was certainly an unnatural thing to give everything to a handyman in lieu of a daughter.

f. Susceptibility to influence

Finally, the court found that although Sophia was strong-willed, she was very susceptible to influence because of her dependence on Wayne as a result of her physical infirmities.

D. Signing Your Will

The signing requirements for a valid will in Oregon are very simple. However, before signing your will, you should also take the following precautions to prevent a claim of undue influence or lack of testamentary capacity.

1. Read the Will

Be sure that you have read your will carefully and that it says precisely what you want it to say. If you do not understand any provision, have it explained to you and satisfy yourself that it is what you want in your will. After all, your will is one of the most personal legal documents you will ever sign.

2. Take Your Time

Do not make any decision in haste that you may later regret. It can be dangerous to have a quick, simple will prepared just before you go on vacation, assuming that it will be a temporary measure until you return. You should always plan your will as if you were going to die the next day.

3. Stay Calm and Alert

Some people use a will to punish a family member for past injuries or insults, and they will do so in a fit of pique. There is nothing illegal about using your will for such purposes. You may disinherit a child or any other family member (except a spouse). But any time you disinherit a family member, you run the risk of a will contest. If you sign your will in haste and anger, you increase the risk that a will contest will be successful.

Try to avoid taking any medication that might affect your alertness when you sign your will. Sometimes there is no way of avoiding signing a will while in the hospital, but hospital and deathbed wills are tempting targets for disinherited heirs.

4. Objective Witnesses

When you sign your will, do not have anyone present who is named as a devisee or beneficiary in the will. Although a beneficiary may be a witness, it is wise to use other people. Do not give anyone a chance to claim undue influence.

5. The Formal Requirements

The most common way to "make" or "sign" your will is for you to sign it in the presence of two or more witnesses. The witnesses must see you sign the will, then, in turn, "attest" the will by signing their names to it. But there are no requirements that you ask the witnesses to sign the will or that the witnesses sign in your presence or that they sign in the presence of each other. There is also no requirement for you to "publish" your will, that is, announce to the witnesses that the document is your will.

A typical testimonium clause, which is the clause that states you have signed your will, reads as follows:

> I have signed this will in Multnomah County, Oregon, on
> May 3, 200- by signing my name on this page of my will,
> which consists of four pages, including this page and
> excluding the affidavit on the following page.

The clause preceding the signatures of the witnesses is called the attestation clause and might read as follows:

> The foregoing will was signed by John Doe, the testator,
> in our presence, and we have signed our names as witnesses
> in Multnomah County, Oregon, on May 3, 200-.

See the example of a will in Sample #2 (on the next page).

There are two additional ways to make a will in Oregon:

(a) Instead of signing the will yourself, you may direct one of the witnesses to sign your name for you. That person should also sign his or her own name and acknowledge that the direction was received from you as the testator. This method would be appropriate if you had some infirmity which made it difficult for you to sign your name.

(b) You may sign your name outside the presence of the two witnesses, and then acknowledge your signature to the two witnesses when they sign. The witnesses must hear you acknowledge your signature, then sign the will themselves.

A will must be in writing, but there is no requirement that it be typed. It can be handwritten or printed. You should date it and initial or sign each page, and sign the last page in full.

Sign only one original. If you sign two originals, and only one is found at your death, it may be presumed that you revoked your will by destroying the missing original. This could invalidate the other original, even if you intended it to be your valid will. After you sign your original, you can make photocopies, which should be clearly marked as copies. To distinguish your original will from copies, sign your original in blue ink or with ink in some color other than black.

A will does not have to be notarized, but it has become common practice to attach a separate affidavit to the will, signed by the witnesses (but not the testator) and notarized, stating that they witnessed the will and that the testator appeared to be of sound mind and over the age of 18.

Sample #2
A Simple Will

Will of John Smith

1. **Declaration**. I, John Smith, declare this my will and revoke all prior wills and codicils. I am a resident of Multnomah County, Oregon, my Social Security number is 000-00-0000, and I was born January 1, 1950.

2. **Heirs**. I am married to Mary Smith. We have three children, John Smith, Jr., who is of legal age, Sarah Smith, born April 10, 1985, and George Smith, born February 14, 1989. Any reference in my will to my children includes not only my children named in my will, but also any afterborn or adopted children of mine.

3. **Personal Representative**. I name as personal representative, to serve without bond, my wife, Mary Smith. If she fails to qualify, or having qualified, ceases to serve, I name Oregon American National Bank as my personal representative.

4. **Disposition of Property**. I give all my property to my wife, Mary Smith. If she fails to survive me, I give all my property, in equal shares, to my children surviving me, and by right of representation, to the issue surviving me of each of my children predeceasing me. If all my children

predecease me, leaving no issue surviving me, I give fifty percent (50%) of the value of my estate to my heirs at law and fifty percent (50%) of the value of my estate to those persons who would have been my wife's heirs at law had she died at the time of my death.

5. **Guardian**. If my wife fails to survive me, I direct that my friends, Ronald and Joyce Peterson, be appointed guardians of any of my children surviving me who are under the age of majority at the time of my death.

6. **Survivorship**. No person named in my will shall be deemed to have survived me unless living on the thirtieth (30th) day after the date of my death.

I have signed this will in Multnomah County, Oregon, on May 3, 200-, by signing my name on this page of my will, which consists of two pages, including this page and excluding the affidavit on the following page.

<u>   John Smith   </u>

The foregoing was signed by John Smith, the testator, in our presence, and we have signed our names as witnesses in Multnomah County, Oregon on May 3, 200-.

<u>   I M Witness   </u>

<u>   U R Witness   </u>

The advantage of having the affidavit signed at the time the will is signed is that, except in the rare case of a will contest, the affidavit avoids having to locate the witnesses after the testator's death, which may be many years after the testator signed the will. The will can be admitted to probate without any testimony from the witnesses other than the affidavit. A will with the attached witness affidavit is known as a "self-proving" will.

No physical disability, such as a visual or hearing impairment, bars a person who has testamentary capacity from making a will. For example, in an early Oregon court decision, the will of a 74-year-old speechless paralytic was challenged. He had testamentary capacity and disposed of his property in his will by giving negative and affirmative replies to questions asked of him. After the will had been written, it was read to him item by item, his assent was given by nodding his head, and after it was read to him, he signed it. The will was valid.

There are two types of wills that are not valid in Oregon:

(a) A holographic will, or a will that is handwritten, dated, and signed by you but not witnessed. All wills must be witnessed to be valid.

(b) A nuncupative will, or an oral will, where you declare or dictate your will before a certain number of witnesses, and it is afterwards put in writing but not signed.

E.   How a Will Is Revoked

1. Marriage

If you marry after you make your will, your marriage automatically revokes your will if you die without redoing your will and your spouse survives you. There are two exceptions to this rule.

(a) If the will indicates an intent that it not be revoked by a subsequent marriage or that it was drafted under circumstances establishing that it was in contemplation of the marriage, then it will not be deemed revoked. An example of this might be where you are contemplating marriage and want to be sure your will is in order before your wedding. This might be done by a provision in the will which reads:

> I am presently engaged to marry to John Smith. I make
> this will expressly in contemplation of my marriage to him,
> and I intend that it not be revoked by such a marriage.

(b) If you and your spouse enter into a contract before the marriage that either makes a provision for your spouse or provides that your spouse shall have no rights in your estate, then the will is not revoked by the marriage. This might happen where both spouses are entering a second marriage and they want to make sure their respective estates are protected for their own children. It is not unusual to enter into a prenuptial or premarital agreement to make those provisions. In this case, a will made prior to marriage would be consistent with such an agreement and would not be revoked by the marriage. Such agreements are discussed in chapter 10.

2. By Annulment or Divorce

A court decree annulling or dissolving a marriage automatically revokes the portions of a will in favor of the former spouse, including a provision naming a former spouse the personal representative. This is done by treating the former spouse as if he or she did not survive the testator. The remainder of the will is still valid.

A provision could be placed in the will stating that the will was made in contemplation of the annulment or marriage dissolution and that the former spouse is to receive his or her share under the will, or act as personal representative in spite of the decree dissolving or annulling the marriage. In that case the subsequent annulment or marriage dissolution would not bar the former spouse from taking his or her share under the will.

There must be a court decree before the spouse is barred from receiving his or her share under a will. This means that if a spouse dies while an annulment or marriage dissolution proceeding is pending but before a decree is entered, the surviving spouse would be entitled to inherit under the deceased spouse's will.

3. By a New Will

A will is revoked by signing a new will, provided either that the new will expressly revokes the prior will or, even without such language, that the new will disposes of all your probate property. A typical provision in a new will might read "I revoke all prior wills and codicils." If a new will does not replace the old will but merely amends it, it is known as a "codicil" and does not revoke the will.

4. By Destruction

You can revoke your will simply by tearing it up and throwing it away, provided that you intend to revoke it by such act. In order for the physical destruction of a will to constitute a valid revocation, you must have the same testamentary capacity and freedom from undue influence that is necessary to make a will. If someone influences you to tear up your will, such revocation is not valid.

You cannot partially revoke your will or amend your will by cutting out portions of it or writing over portions of it. It is an all-or-nothing rule. If you intend to revoke your will or to amend it, do not write on it. If you want to change it, see your attorney and make a new will or a codicil. If you intend to revoke your will in its entirety and do not want a new will, then tear it up, burn it, or destroy it so that there is no question of your intent. Otherwise, whatever you intended very possibly will not be fulfilled and will probably lead to litigation. Either the entire will is considered revoked, or the entire will is considered valid. Partial revocation is not possible.

For example, Nellie made pen and pencil marks on 17 of the 22 paragraphs in her will. The court held that she intended to revoke her will and held it invalid.

In another case, Ella cut out or crossed through various paragraphs of her will. There was testimony at a trial that she wanted to give her estate to various religious and charitable organizations and was crossing out or excluding just her relatives. But the court held that she intended to revoke her entire will, so her estate went to her relatives and not to the charities.

In another case, Charles attempted to cancel certain paragraphs of his will by drawing lines through those paragraphs with his pen and writing that he was canceling them. He also wrote in three additions to the will. The court ruled that there can be no partial revocation, held the will valid and admitted it to probate as originally written before Charles' changes, even though his intent was clear that he wanted to make the changes indicated.

F.   Agreements Concerning Wills

It is possible to make a binding contract with another person relating to your will. For example, you can agree to:

(a) make your will in a certain way,

(b) give or devise certain property to a person,

(c) not revoke or change your will or devise, or

(d) die intestate; in other words, a contract not to make a will.

If you breach the contract, the other person can sue you or your estate.

A typical situation for such an agreement is a contract between a husband and wife, particularly in a second marriage where the spouses want to protect the children of a prior marriage (see chapter 10). Another common contract is a promise to devise in exchange for services rendered.

At one time it was common for a married couple to include both their wills in one document. This was known as a joint, mutual, or reciprocal will. Joint wills led to much litigation over whether or not, after the first spouse's death, the surviving spouse could revoke the will. Such wills are rare today.

For joint wills executed after January 1, 1974, Oregon law provides that the writing of a joint will does not create a presumption of a contract not to revoke the will after the death of one of the spouses. Any contract relating to a will made after January 1, 1974 must be indicated in writing either in—

(a) provisions of a will stating the material provisions of the contract, or

(b) an express reference in a will to a contract and evidence outside the will proving the terms of the contract, or

(c) a written statement signed by the deceased evidencing the contract.

G.   Wills Signed in Other States

What if you signed a will while a resident in another state and then moved to Oregon? Your will is still valid in Oregon, provided that it is signed and complies with the formalities of the state where you resided at the time you signed it or, if you signed it in a state other than the state of your residence, it complies with the formalities of the state where you signed it.

Nevertheless, if you move to Oregon from another state, you should have a new will drafted by an Oregon attorney, partly because there will be matters of Oregon law other than the formalities of signing that may require different provisions in your will, and partly because, upon your death, it may be easier to prove your will with Oregon witnesses.

If you sign a will in Oregon and then move to another state, your Oregon will may or may not be valid in that state, depending on that state's laws. You should therefore have a new will drawn up by an attorney in the state to which you move.

H.   Where to Keep Your Will

There is no government agency in Oregon that will store your will for you while you are alive. Consider storing your will in one of the locations described below.

1. Safe Deposit Box

A safe deposit box at a financial institution is the best place to keep your will. This is the place where there is the least risk that your will can be destroyed by fire or other natural disaster, lost, stolen or misplaced. Because it is the most customary place to keep a will, it is the most likely place for your family to look for your will after your death.

2. Trust Company

If you name a trust company as first or second choice of personal representative or as trustee in your will, the trust company may store your will for you at no cost as a courtesy to you.

3. At Home

Many people prefer storing their wills at home. If this is your preference, you should keep it in a fireproof safe or file, or, if you do not have one, then in some other relatively fireproof location, such as your freezer (in a waterproof container).

4. Attorney's Office

Some attorneys store their client's wills for them in their firm's safe deposit box. You should give this alternative careful thought before selecting it. It may be difficult for you to ask the attorney for your will if you later want to change attorneys. Also, the personal representative should have the option to choose an attorney to help probate your estate after you die. He or she may feel pressured to use the attorney who is storing your will. Even if there is a provision in your will that directs the personal representative to hire a particular attorney, the personal representative is not bound to do so.

If an attorney stores your will and he or she dies, retires, leaves the practice of law, or moves out of state, it may be difficult for you or your personal representative to locate your will.

5. With Other People

Some people prefer their personal representative or some close relative to store their will. This is not a problem if the personal representative is a trust company. But if you name an individual and that person keeps it at home, there is always the risk of fire, theft, and misplacement. Also, if the individual stores your will in a safe deposit box and dies before you do, the contents of your will may be disclosed to strangers.

Regardless of where you store your will, make sure it can be located after your death. If your will cannot be found after your death, there is a good chance that it will not be admitted to probate and will not control the disposition of your probate property.

You can improve the chances of your will being found by—

(a) keeping a copy of your will at home with your other important papers and noting the location of the original,

(b) noting the location of the will in a letter of instructions,

(c) informing your personal representative of the location of the will or the location of the letter of instructions,

(d) having your personal representative as a co-lessee of the safe deposit box, and

(e) informing relatives, friends, or clergy either of the location of the will or of the letter of instructions.

I.   Letter of Instructions

One of the main reasons for the sometimes lengthy delay in starting a probate is the disarray in which most people leave their property and financial affairs. This delay can cause unnecessary expense to the estate by allowing defaults on obligations to creditors and extra interest and service charges. It may also lead to hardship for persons who were dependent on the decedent for support.

You can minimize these risks by organizing your personal and financial affairs, both for yourself and for your personal representative, with the preparation of a letter of instructions. This letter should contain the following:

(a) A list of all your property and debts.

(b) The location of all important documents relating to your estate, such as your will, life insurance policies, pension, documents, etc.

(c) The location of your safe deposit box and the safe deposit key.

(d) The names, addresses, and telephone numbers of your professional advisors, including your accountant, attorney, life insurance agent, stockbroker, trust officer, or financial counselor. If you want your personal representative to use the services of these particular advisors, note this in your letter, not in your will.

(e) Instructions concerning your funeral, burial, or cremation wishes. You may want to include a list of friends and relatives who should be contacted at your death, particularly if they live out of town and may not hear about your death right away.

(f) The names, addresses, and relationships of those relatives who would have been your heirs had you died without a will, and the dates of birth of any minor heirs. This information will be necessary for your personal representative to have immediately at your death.

(g) The names and addresses of all devisees under your will or beneficiaries under any trust agreement if they are not heirs.

(h) Your birth date, place of birth, Social Security Number, and the names of your father and mother (including mother's maiden name) and whether or not you are a veteran.

(i) Special instructions to your personal representative explaining how to divide up your furniture or other tangible property.

(j) The reasons for omitting an heir from your will. Such instructions will serve only as a guide; they will not be binding.

(k) Once you have completed, dated, and signed your letter of instructions, you should put one copy with your original will, keep another copy with a copy of your will at home in a place that is easy to find after your death, and give one copy (in a sealed envelope to ensure confidentiality) to your personal representative, your attorney, and any other close personal advisor. As an alternative, give them a letter, to be opened at your death, telling them where to find your letter of instructions.

J.   Review Your Will and Estate Plan

Once you have signed your will, you should not put it away and forget about it for the next 20 years. A will can become outdated because of changes in your marital status, the death of a beneficiary, a substantial increase or decrease in the size of your estate, a move to another state or country, or a change in the law. It is a good idea to review all your documents, your financial inventory, and your letter of instructions once a year or on some other regular basis.

K.   Safe Deposit Boxes

A safe deposit box is the best place to store your will, trust or other original estate planning documents as well as other documents which are hard to replace, such as a marriage license or birth certificate. Many financial institutions lease safe deposit boxes to the public. The person renting the box is generally called the lessee.

Many people believe that a safe deposit box is "frozen" or "sealed" when the person leasing the box dies. This is not true in Oregon. At one time, the Oregon Department of Revenue had the right to inventory the contents of a safe deposit box when the lessee died, for inheritance tax purposes, but that law was repealed some years ago.

You should always have at least two persons listed as lessees of the box. For a married couple, both spouses should sign as lessees. For a single person, consider naming your personal representative or successor trustee of your living trust as a joint lessee.

This will assure easy access to the box when a person dies. You can also authorize an agent under a financial power of attorney to have access to the box if you are incapacitated.

If there are two or more lessees, and one dies, the other lessee has immediate right of access to the box and can remove a will, trust agreement or other contents. However, if the sole lessee or the last surviving lessee of a box dies, financial institutions are required to follow a uniform procedure in granting access to a safe deposit box.

Only persons who have a legitimate interest in the decedent's affairs can gain access to the box at the decedent's death. They are the personal representative named in the decedent's will, the surviving spouse or other heir, a guardian, conservator, trustee or agent under a power of attorney from the decedent, or a person the decedent designated in a writing filed with the financial institution. The person must furnish a death certificate or other evidence of death and an affidavit to the financial institution.

The box can be opened only for the limited purposes of doing a will or trust agreement search, to search for documents relating to the disposition of the decedent's remains, or to inventory the contents. If there is a will, the financial institution will release the will to the personal representative, or if the personal representative cannot be found, will file the will with the probate court. A trust agreement will be released to the person who is to succeed as trustee at the decedent's death. A copy of any instructions relating to disposition of the decedent's remains will be released to the person submitting the affidavit.

Oregon's law does not speak to the disposition of the other contents of the safe deposit box. Generally the financial institution will release the contents solely to the personal representative of the decedent's estate, once appointed, to the claiming successor under Oregon's small estate affidavit, or to another authorized person.

Chapter 8

Planning Your Will

Your right to dispose of your property at death is a valuable incident of ownership. This has been described by Oregon's courts as a "sacred and inviolable" right of your absolute dominion over your property. As part of that right, you are entitled to give your property to whomever you please and without regard to the natural or legitimate claims of your heirs. While you cannot totally disinherit a spouse under Oregon law, you can favor your lover over your spouse and give your lover more than your spouse, or you can completely disinherit a child, and this in no way makes your will invalid. There is no "reasonably prudent man's standard" as is applied in other areas of law. As one Oregon court has stated:

> No man is bound to make a will in such a manner as to
> deserve approbation from the prudent, the wise, or the good.
> A testator is permitted to be capricious or improvident, and
> is, moreover, at liberty to conceal the circumstances and the
> motives by which he has been actuated in his deposition.

Whether or not you exercise your right is up to you. If you do not exercise your right, then the state exercises that right for you and disposes of your probate property at death as outlined in chapter 6. You should always plan your will as if you were going to die the day after you sign it. If you do not treat your will and estate planning that way, then the state of Oregon will do it for you.

A will must reflect your intentions very clearly, because when the question of your intent becomes important, you are no longer around to explain to anyone what you meant. A good will is not only clear and concise, it also tries to cover the various contingencies that can occur between the time you sign the will and the time of your death. It is particularly important that the will cover the possibility that one or more of the devisees you name in your will may die before you do, or that property that you specifically mention in your will is no longer owned by you at your death.

A. The Opening Clause

A simple opening clause might read:

> I, JOHN SMITH, declare this my will and revoke all prior wills and codicils. I am a resident of Multnomah County, Oregon, my Social Security Number is 000-00-0000, and I was born January 1, 1950.

This clause serves several functions.

(a) It indicates that you intend the document to be your will. You do not need to say "last will and testament." You do not have to state that you are of sound and disposing mind, which is common in many wills. Such a statement does not prove that in fact you are of sound and disposing mind. There are better ways of showing that.

(b) It is important to expressly revoke all prior wills and codicils. You should do so even if you do not remember ever having signed a will before. You may have forgotten that you did. Of course, if you are amending a prior will rather than redoing it entirely, such language would be inappropriate.

(c) You should declare that you are a resident of the state of Oregon. Your place of residence, or domicile, is a matter of your intent as reflected by such indicia as the state where you register to vote, where you file income tax returns, where you register your car titles, and where you spend a majority of your time. The laws of the state of your domicile determine how your will is interpreted and how your estate is taxed.

B. Your Heirs

An heirship clause in a will might read:

> On the date of my will, my only heirs are my wife, Mary
> Smith, and our three children, John Smith, Jr., who is of legal
> age, Sarah Smith, born April 10, 1985, and George Smith,
> born February 14, 1989.

An heirship clause serves several purposes.

(a) Naming your heirs in your will is a good way to show that you
have testamentary capacity when you sign your will. Be sure
you are accurate; if you make mistakes identifying your heirs,
that might suggest you lack testamentary capacity.

(b) An heirship clause is also helpful to your personal representative, who must notify all your heirs that you have died and your
will has been admitted to probate. Your personal representative
must notify your heirs of your death, even though you disinherit
them, that is, make no provision for them in your will.

(c) If you have children, listing them in your will will help your
personal representative decide whether or not you intentionally
or accidentally omitted any child born to you or adopted by you
after you sign your will. Such children are known as "pretermitted children." The basic rules are as follows:

　(i)　If you have one or more children at the time you sign your
will and make no provision in your will for your children,
then an after-born or adopted child will not be included in
your will.

　(ii)　If you do have children at the time you sign the will and
make provisions for them in your will, then any afterborn or
adopted child will be entitled to share equally in the shares
of your estate you give your children.

　(iii) If you have no children at the time you sign the will, and
thereafter a child is born to or adopted by you, then that
child is entitled to the share to which it would be entitled
under the laws of intestate succession.

(iv) These rules do not apply to or include stepchildren or foster children.

(d) Listing the dates of birth of children is helpful when they are minors, since this will indicate to the personal representative whether such children are minors at the time of your death and may need a guardian or conservator. Listing dates of birth can also be helpful to your personal representative if you establish a trust for your children which provides that they are to receive their share of the trust at a certain age, say 25.

(e) If you intend to disinherit a child or other heir, name the heir and state your intention. This way, there can be no question about your intent and no basis for a claim that you inadvertently omitted a particular heir. You can add words such as "I expressly make no provision in my will for my son, Charles."

Consider explaining your reasons for the disinheritance in a separate letter addressed to the disinherited heir and leave the letter with your will. This way your reasons do not become part of the public record when your will is admitted to probate.

A letter of explanation can serve several purposes. For instance, suppose you are giving one child a larger share of your estate than you are giving your other children because the favored child is struggling financially and the other children are financially secure, a form of partial disinheritance. A letter of explanation can minimize the risk of misunderstanding and hard feelings among your children, misunderstanding that they will have to live with for the rest of their lives, because you are not treating them equally and they do not know why. Better yet, discuss your reasons with your children while you are alive.

A letter of explanation can also be helpful if you are disinheriting a child from whom you are estranged. The letter of explanation will be helpful to your personal representative if the estranged child contests the will. Also consider including a "no contest" clause in your will (see page 107).

There is a common misconception that you must leave one dollar to each heir you disinherit. This is not true. Leaving a dollar to a disinherited heir will only cause complications for your personal representative, who will have to treat the heir as a devisee under your will, give the heir notice to which he or she would not otherwise be entitled, and distribute the one dollar to the heir.

There are two exceptions to the rule that you can disinherit all your heirs:

(i)   You may partially, but not totally, disinherit your spouse.

(ii) Your spouse and dependent children are entitled to support from your estate during probate. Even disinherited children are entitled to support during probate if they are dependents. This could last up to two years and possibly use up all your probate property.

C.   Personal Representative

The personal representative is the person you name in your will to handle the administration of your estate when you die. It can be an individual such as a close relative, a trusted advisor such as your attorney or accountant, or a trust company.

Individuals who are not qualified to act as a personal representative include incompetents, persons under age 18, suspended or disbarred attorneys, judges of Oregon courts and licensed funeral service practitioners. A convicted felon may act as a personal representative unless the court finds that the reasons for his or her conviction are similar to the grounds for removal of a personal representative and that it is likely that the person will be unfaithful or neglectful of his or her duties as a personal representative.

Select your personal representative the same way you select a trustee (see chapter 4). You will want to consider the same qualities of professional management, impartiality, perpetual existence, integrity, solvency, and cost. However, several unique factors need to be considered in choosing a personal representative.

(a) Trust companies are in the business of settling estates. They are not required to file a personal representative's bond. A trust company, of course, will take its statutory fee for acting as personal representative and will seek additional fees for extraordinary services. Attorney fees should be lower when a trust company rather than an individual acts as personal representative because the trust company will handle many of the responsibilities for its statutory fee that an attorney would handle and charge for if an individual were the personal representative. On the other hand, frequently an individual personal representative who is also a devisee under the will waives the personal representative fee or takes a reduced fee.

(b) You may name two or more personal representatives. For instance, if you have two children and you want to treat them equally for all purposes under your will, you can name them both as personal representatives. Or you can name your accountant or other professional adviser jointly with a child to ensure adequate professional attention to the administration of your estate. Naming two personal representatives may make administration of an estate more cumbersome, however, because all steps require the concurrence of both.

(c) You may name a personal representative who is a devisee under the will. In a husband-wife situation, the surviving spouse is the logical choice. He or she will normally work very closely with and be advised by the attorney.

(d) You can name your attorney. However, the personal representative has many responsibilities, such as cleaning out a house and getting it ready for sale, or disposing of the personal effects or paying routine bills, that do not require a lawyer's expertise or justify a lawyer's fee. It may be cheaper to let the attorney act solely as attorney for the personal representative and select some other person whose hourly rate is not as high.

(e) Wills commonly waive the requirement that a personal representative post a bond to protect creditors and devisees of the estate. Without a waiver provision, the personal representative is required to be bonded, usually with a commercial surety bond. Such bonds have an annual premium calculated at the rate of about $5 per $1,000 of value of assets. Thus, a $50,000 estate might require a bond costing $250 or more per year. If you trust an individual enough to ask that individual to be your personal representative, you had better trust him or her enough to serve without bond. Otherwise, name a trust company as your personal representative.

(f) Always name one or more alternative personal representatives in case your first choice dies before you do or during the course of probate, declines to act, resigns, or is removed. This is especially important if you are naming an individual rather than a trust company as your personal representative, but it is also advisable where you name a trust company as first choice. Sometimes a trust company may decline to serve. You can name an individual as first choice and a trust company as second choice.

D. When You Own Real Property in Another State

If you are an Oregon resident with real property in another state, your estate may require a separate probate in the other state. This is called "ancillary administration." Ancillary administration ensures that your non-Oregon real property is distributed according to your will. Your intangible personal property, wherever located, and your real and tangible personal property located in Oregon, will be probated by an Oregon probate court. Make certain that your Oregon personal representative can act in the state where your real property is located. If not, name an ancillary personal representative in your will who can serve. Make sure that your will complies with the laws of the state where your real property is located.

E. How to Make Gifts in Your Will

There are three types of gifts of property in a will: a specific devise, a general devise, and the residue.

1. Specific Devise

A specific devise is a devise of a specific thing or specific part of your estate. Examples of a specific devise are a gift of your rings and jewelry, or your house, or the balance in your savings account to a certain person or charity.

2. General Devise

A general devise is a devise chargeable generally against your probate property. For instance, if you give a gift of $1,000 to a grandson, this means that you do not care where it comes from in your estate, as long as your grandson receives the $1,000.

This may be contrasted with a specific devise in which you give whatever funds are in your checking account at the time of your death. Such a gift would constitute a specific devise. Generally, because checking and savings account balances can fluctuate in amount, or you may move the funds to a different bank, it is better to give a specific dollar amount rather than the balance in an account.

3. Residue

The residue of your estate is all your probate property remaining after your general and specific devises and after payment of all expense, taxes and claims. The clause disposing of the residue of your estate may be the most important clause in your will.

You do not need to make specific or general devises. For example, your will could read in its entirety "I give all my estate in equal shares to my children."

However, if you do not have a clause disposing of the residue of your estate (or all of your estate if you have no specific or general devises), then the probate property you do not mention and specifically devise will be distributed to your heirs outside your will and according to the laws of intestate succession.

Because you cannot predict what probate property you will own at your death, it is important to use the terms "residue" or "residuary estate," rather than trying to list every item of probate property you own. The use of the term "residue" gives you absolute assurance that none of your probate property will pass outside your will by intestate succession.

You may give the residue of your estate in equal shares or by percentages. For instance, if you want to distribute it in unequal shares you might give 50% of the residue to one child, 25% to another child, and 12-1/2% each to two grandchildren. In this way, you will ensure that distribution will be made in terms of the value of your assets at the time of your death and that you will dispose of all your probate estate.

A simple will containing all three types of devises might read as follows:

(a) I give my house and my car to my son Michael. (A specific devise.)

(b) I give the sum of $50,000 to my daughter Alice. (A general devise.)

(c) I give the residue to my daughter Barbara.

F. Planning Specific and General Devises

Specific devises and general devises require special planning. For example, if you give all your probate property in equal shares to your children, it does not normally matter how you allocate funeral expenses, taxes, or administration expenses. When the estate is settled, each child will receive an equal share of what is left after all expenses, taxes and claims are paid. But if you give specific or general devises, planning becomes a little more complicated.

These are some of the things you should consider about specifically devised property:

(a) What happens if you sell your house on contract after you sign the will but it has not been paid off when you die? Who receives the balance due on the contract?

(b) Who receives insurance proceeds if the house is destroyed by fire shortly before you die?

(c) Out of what assets does the personal representative pay the mortgage? The funeral bill? The debts and administration costs?

(d) Who receives the income from rental property during probate?

Careful planning can cover each of these areas in your will. However, if you do not plan, specific rules will determine what happens.

G. What if Property Is Sold or Destroyed?

If you specifically devise property to someone, and you sell it before you die, the specific devise fails, and the devisee receives neither the property nor its equivalent value. This is known as the doctrine of ademption by extinction. Simply put, you cannot give away in your will what you do not own at your death.

A special statute, however, modifies this rule by providing for "nonademption" of specific devises in certain situations. In these situations, the property does not "adeem" and the devisee still receives something.

1. Damaged Property

If specifically devised property is destroyed or damaged, and it is insured, the specific devisee is entitled to any insurance proceeds paid to your personal representative after your death, together with a cash payment, equal to the amount of insurance proceeds that you received during the six months preceding your death. If the property is not insured, the devise fails.

2. Sale of Property

If you sell specifically devised real property under a land sales contract, the specific devisee receives title to the property. The devisee will receive the property subject to a contractual obligation to convey title to the buyer when the buyer pays off the contract. In effect, the specific devisee receives the right to collect the balance due on the contract and a security interest in the property.

If you sell specifically devised real property by any other method or if you sell personal property, the specific devisee is entitled to the balance of the purchase price unpaid at death, any interest accrued but unpaid at death, any security interest in the property securing the obligation, and a general pecuniary devise equal to the amount of the purchase price paid to you within six months before your death.

If a guardian or conservator is appointed for you and sells specifically devised property or receives insurance proceeds or a condemnation award relating to such property, the specific devisee is entitled to the proceeds from such sale, the insurance proceeds, or the condemnation award. This rule applies even if the property is sold more than six months before your death.

3. Condemnation

If specifically devised property is taken by condemnation before your death, the specific devisee is entitled to the amount of the condemnation award unpaid at your death plus a general pecuniary devise equal to the amount of the award paid to you during the six months prior to your death. Your property is condemned when the state or other governmental agency forces you to sell your property to it for some public purpose such as a highway or park.

4. Stocks and Bonds

If you specifically devise stocks, bonds, or other securities, and receive additional or substituted shares after the date of your will, the specific devise is considered to include the additional or substituted securities. This rule would apply to stock dividends, stock splits, mergers, reorganizations and similar transactions.

H.   Mortgages and Other Encumbrances

Specifically devised property may have a mortgage or other encumbrances against it. An encumbrance is any claim against the property that constitutes a lien and a cloud on the title and represents an obligation to some person, organization, or government agency secured by the property. The law divides encumbrances into two categories:

(a) Voluntary encumbrances, such as mortgages, trust deeds, security agreements, pledges, public improvement assessment liens, or contract liens; and

(b) Involuntary encumbrances, such as judgments and tax liens.

A specific devisee must assume and pay any voluntary encumbrances, but the residuary devisees will have to pay any involuntary encumbrances.

A specific devisee has two options with a voluntary encumbrance:

(a) Require the personal representative to apply any rents or profits received from the property to the encumbrance

(b) Request the personal representative to satisfy the encumbrance out of specifically devised property

You may modify these rules by directing that the specifically devised property be given to the devisees free and clear of any encumbrances.

I. Who Pays the Bills?

There are several categories of expenses that must be paid after a person's death and during the administration of an estate. The principal ones are the following:

(a) Debt owed by the deceased as of the date of death including expenses of last illness and income taxes.

(b) Funeral expenses, attorney and personal representative fees, court costs, and other administration expenses.

(c) Expenses relating to a specific devise, such as mortgage payments, property taxes, and repairs.

(d) Inheritance or estate taxes (death taxes).

The personal representative is not required to make any payments on a mortgage or other voluntary encumbrances against specifically devised property except from rents and profits received from the property. Property taxes, insurance and repairs are paid first out of the income from the property. If the income is not adequate to pay all the expenses, the remaining expenses are treated like any other administration expense, but the personal representative has a lien against the property for payment of a voluntary encumbrance.

Debts of the deceased and funeral and administration expenses are paid out of property in the following order:

(a) Property not disposed of by the will (This will rarely happen if a person has a will. It means that the person would have had to die partially intestate with part of the probate property going to the heirs).

(b) Out of the residue. Normally all debts and expenses are paid out of the residue.

(c) If the residue is not sufficient to pay all debts and expense, out of the general devises.

(d) If the residue and general devises are not sufficient, out of the specific devises.

This is called the order of abatement. Abatement is proportionate within each class of devise. For example, if you provide that one half of the residue goes to each of two different persons, then each person's share of the residue abates, or must bear its one-half share, to the extent of one-half of the expenses.

These rules apply regardless of any provision in your will directing your personal representative to pay your "just debts." By law, your personal representative is required to pay your legal obligations and the expenses of administration, even if your will does not have this provision.

J.   Who Pays Death Taxes

The Oregon inheritance tax, the federal estate tax, and any other applicable state inheritance taxes, if any (death taxes), are apportioned among all beneficiaries, probate and nonprobate, in proportion to the value of their interests in the estate.

For example, if you died owning life insurance and jointly owned property plus probate property, the beneficiary of the insurance policy, the surviving joint owner and each devisee under the will would each have to pay a proportionate share of the death taxes. The personal representative files the death tax returns, and nonprobate property owners pay their share of the death taxes to the personal representative.

This rule can be changed by a provision in your will directing that death taxes be paid out of a certain part of your estate, typically the residue. This may be important if you make specific devises and want to make sure that such devisees receive the property undiminished by death taxes. For instance, in the example in section E., (page 97) Michael would have to come up with funds to pay his share of the death taxes on the house and car, and Alice's $50,000 gift would be reduced by its share of death taxes unless you had a tax apportionment clause which read the all death taxes on probate property are to be paid out of the residue. A typical clause might read as follows:

> Death Taxes: My personal representative shall pay all estate, inheritance, succession, and transfer taxes, plus interest and penalties (death taxes), which become payable by reason of my death in respect of any property passing under my will, out of the residue of my estate as an expense of administration and without apportionment and shall not prorate or charge them against any specific or general devises under my will. Death taxes on property passing outside my will shall be apportioned in the manner provided by law.

K.   Who Receives the Income During Probate?

The administration of an estate in Oregon will take from six months to more than two years. Who receives the income generated from the probate property during that period of time?

The income is not used to pay expenses in settling the estate, such as debts, funeral expenses, and administration expenses. Those are a charge against the probate property.

Specific devisees are entitled to the income from the property devised to them less taxes, ordinary repairs, and other expenses of operation and management of the property.

General pecuniary devisees, such as a devisee entitled to $10,000, do not share in the income during probate. But if they are not paid within one year after the personal representative is appointed, they are entitled to interest at the rate of 5% per annum for a period beginning one year after the appointment of the personal representative. The interest is paid out of the residue.

Residuary devisees receive all the other income.

L.   Your Tangible Personal Property

If you are giving your furniture, furnishings, personal belongings and other tangible personal property to more than one person, you may find it cumbersome to list every article of property and figure out who will receive it. You may also change your mind or give it away or buy additional personal property so that the list quickly becomes outdated.

There are several ways to dispose of your personal property. For instance, if you are giving it to all your children, and they are old enough to make their own choices, you can provide that they may divide it among themselves as they may mutually agree, but if they cannot agree within some time period, for instance 90 days, then the personal representative will decide how to divide it. There are several other ways to handle this type of property, particularly if your children are minors. You can do one of the following:

(a) Direct the personal representative to divide the tangible personal property among your children in as nearly equal shares as possible in terms of value, taking into account whatever wishes each child expresses for a particular article. If the personal property cannot be divided equally, direct your personal representative to distribute cash to the child receiving the lesser value in order to equalize by value.

(b) Give your personal representative discretion to decide how to divide your personal property, and in addition, give your personal representative a memorandum directing how you would like to see it divided among your children. You can also state in your will that you know the personal representative will distribute the property in accordance with your wishes. This would be considered "precatory," which means that your wishes are not legally binding, but that you are trusting your personal representative to distribute it as you wish. The benefit of this arrangement is that you can update your list from time to time without amending your will.

(c) Give a trusted friend or relative the authority, known as a limited power of appointment, to distribute all your tangible personal property. Such a clause might be appropriate where the personal representative is a bank or a person who would not be aware of your desires or understand or know your children well enough to make a reasonable division of the personal property.

(e) If you want a legally binding direction for distribution of specific items of personal property, but do not want to incorporate or include the entire list in your will, you can incorporate a list by reference. However, the list of personal property must be dated and in existence prior to the date of the will to make it binding on the personal representative. If you intend later to update the list, then you will have to re-execute the will to make the list binding.

M. What if a Devisee Dies Before You Do?

In Oregon, if a devisee dies before the testator and that person is related by blood or adoption to the testator and, in addition, leaves lineal descendants, then the descendants take the devisee's gift by representation. Thus, if you make a gift of $1,000 to a sister, and she dies before you do, leaving two children of her own, each child would receive $500. If there are no descendants, the gift would lapse and become a part of the residue. This is known as the antilapse law. This rule applies even if you make no provision in your will naming alternate devisees if a primary devisee fails to survive you.

This law will give some protection to cover such a contingency, providing that you are giving your probate property to relatives and that this result reflects your desires. However, it is better for you to provide specifically for disposition of your property in case one or more devisees die before you do.

To a certain extent, you have to play the odds in this situation. For instance, if you have two or more children and they have children of their own, there is little likelihood that all your children and grandchildren will die before both you and your spouse.

However, such contingency planning becomes more important if you have only one child. Suppose that child died before both you and your spouse and had no children of his or her own, and you made no provision in your will for such a contingency. What would happen to your estate? It would depend on the accident of who died first, you or your spouse.

If you died first, and then your spouse died leaving no children and with no other provision in his or her will, then all the estate would go to his or her heirs at law, which would be the parents if living, otherwise brothers and sisters or other heirs. If your spouse died before you did, then everything would go to your heirs at law upon your subsequent death.

To minimize this risk, you could provide that if such a situation were to occur, one-half of the estate would go to your side of the family and one-half to your spouse's side of the family, and each of your wills would contain identical provisions, so that the accident of who died first would not determine who received your estate. A typical provision might read:

> If my wife fails to survive me, and if all my children
> predecease me, leaving no issue surviving me, I give 50% of
> my estate to my heirs at law and 50% of my estate to those
> persons who would have been my wife's heirs at law had she
> died at the time of my death.

Another possibility is to give all or part of your estate to charity.

N. Survivorship

If a devisee under your will dies at the same time or shortly after you die, that devisee is deemed to have died before you unless it is established by clear and convincing evidence that the devisee survived you by at least 120 hours (the equivalent of five days). This rule minimizes the need to establish order of deaths in simultaneous death situations such as a common auto or airplane accident, and may eliminate the need to probate the estate of a devisee who dies shortly after you do.

You can provide for a substantially longer period of time than five days. However, if you set too long a period of time, commencement of probate proceedings may be delayed because there is no way to determine who the devisees of your will are until the survivorship period has elapsed. A 30-day survivorship clause is a reasonable compromise.

Such a provision might read as follows:

> No person named in my will shall be deemed to have
> survived me unless it is established by clear and convincing
> evidence that the person survived me by at least 720 hours.

In a large estate, the presumption of survivorship in case of simultaneous deaths may be reversed for death tax purposes. Such a clause might state that if you and your spouse die simultaneously and the order of death cannot be established, your spouse will be deemed to have survived you. Such a clause may make sense if you have an estate subject to federal estate tax and your spouse has only a modest estate. By reversing the presumption that your spouse predeceased you, it will be possible for your estates to take advantage of both estate tax exemptions ($1 million in 2002) in case of simultaneous or near-simultaneous deaths.

For instance, suppose a married couple has an estate of $2 million, $1.5 million owned by the wife and $500,000 by husband. Their living trusts or wills provide that on the first death, an amount equal to the federal estate tax exemption will go into a bypass trust for the surviving spouse, and the balance outright to the surviving spouse. They both die in 2002 in an airplane crash. If their trusts or wills followed the statutory presumption, then the husband would be presumed to have survived the wife, the wife's $1.5 million estate would pass directly to the children, the husband's $500,000 estate would also pass directly to their children, and they would not have fully utilized the husband's $1 million exemption.

If in their trusts or wills, they had reversed the order of survivorship, then the husband would have been presumed to have survived the wife, $500,000 of the wife's estate would have been distributed to the husband's estate, and his estate would then distribute $1 million to their children, thus fully utilizing his $1 million exemption.

O. Guardian

If you have children who are minors (any unmarried child under the age of 18), then you should provide in your will for the appointment of a guardian in case both you and your spouse die while one or more of your children are minors.

The function of a guardian is to take the place of a deceased parent in caring for the minor, including facilitating the minor's educational, social, and other activities, authorizing medical or other professional care, and deciding other matters relating to the minor's physical and mental well-being.

A guardian is appointed by the court in a guardianship proceedings, and the court is required to appoint the person most suitable for taking care of the minor. A request that a certain person be appointed guardian of your minor children must be taken into account by the court, but the court is not bound by your designation. However, unless the person you choose as guardian is unsuitable to take care of your children, the court will appoint that person.

The will is a good place to put your designation or selection of guardian. However, this is not the only place that you can indicate your selection. You can write a letter, sign an affidavit, or state in some other document whom you wish the court to appoint as the guardian.

If the parents of a minor child are not living together, and the parent having custody of the child dies, the surviving parent does not have an automatic right to custody or appointment as guardian. However, a court will not grant custody and guardianship rights to some other person, such as a stepparent or grandparent, even if that person has established a child-parent relationship with the child, solely because it is in the best interest of the child. A court must give significant weight to the right of the surviving parent to the care, custody and control of the child.

If you are a parent with custody of a minor child, and the child's other parent is still alive, your designation of a person other than the other parent as guardian for the child will normally not be effective. However, you should still name your choice of guardian for your child in the event the other parent dies before you do or does not want custody, or in the rare chance that a court were to rule that the other parent is not entitled to custody

P. No Contest Clause

Whenever you disinherit a child or treat your children differently in your will, you should take steps to assure that the disinherited or disfavored child does not contest your will. This recommendation also applies if you have no children and are disinheriting a grandchild, nephew or niece, or some other heir, that is, a person who would have inherited from you if you did not have a will.

One way to head off a contest is to have an open discussion with all your children or other heirs and explain your reasons for the disparate treatment of your children or other heirs. You should also leave a detailed letter of explanation with your will, to be opened in case of a contest.

Another step you can take is to include an "in terrorem" or "no contest" clause in your will, which states that if the disfavored child or other devisee challenges your will, that devisee will forfeit the share of the estate which you left to the devisee. To make the clause effective, you will have to leave a large enough share of your estate to the disfavored child or other devisee so as to discourage the devisee from challenging the will by giving the devisee too much to lose if the challenge fails.

An in terrorem clause is valid in Oregon and will be enforced by the courts with two exceptions: (1) the devisee establishes that the devisee has probable cause to believe the will is a forgery or has been revoked; or (2) the will contest is brought by a fiduciary, such as a guardian or conservator, acting on behalf of a minor or an incapacitated adult.

Chapter 9

Simultaneous Deaths, Slayers, and Disclaimers

Survivorship is a critical factor in determining who gets your property at your death. As a general rule, if a devisee under your will, the beneficiary of your life insurance policy, or the other co-owner of your joint and survivorship property survives you, that person receives the property you left to him or her. If that person does not survive you, he or she does not receive the property.

Oregon has special laws to determine the order of survivorship in those situations where two persons who each have an interest in the same property die within a short period of time of each other.

A.   Simultaneous Deaths

The basic rule is that if the right of a person to receive certain property is conditioned on surviving someone else, and both people die simultaneously or near simultaneously, then the intended recipient of the property will be deemed to have died first. The only exception is if it is established by clear and convincing evidence that the intended recipient of the property survived the other person by at least 120 hours, or five days. For instance, suppose you give some property in your will to a favorite nephew and you both die in the same car accident. The property will be distributed as if the nephew had died first unless the nephew's personal representative can establish that the nephew survived you by at least 120 hours.

The reason for the 120-hour survivorship requirement and the requirement of a high standard of proof of survivorship is to eliminate disputes over survivorship in common tragedies where both persons die before any other person arrives at the scene and the only way to prove survivorship is through gruesome medical evidence.

This rule of survivorship applies to any property interest where the recipient of the property must survive to receive the property, including the following:

(a) heirs of a person dying with probate property and without a will;

(b) devisees of a person dying with probate property and with a will;

(c) beneficiaries of an insured under an insurance policy;

(d) beneficiaries of an annuitant under an annuity contract;

(e) beneficiaries of an owner of an account at a financial institution or a security held in ITF (in trust for), POD (payable on death), or TOD (transferable on death) ownership;

(f) beneficiaries of an owner or participant of an IRA (individual retirement account) or other retirement account;

(g) beneficiaries of a trustor of a living trust.

If two people owning property in a form of joint and survivorship ownership die simultaneously, half the property will be distributed as if one had survived and half as if the other had survived. In one Oregon case, for example, a married couple died in a common boat accident. They had owned all their property jointly with right of survivorship, and neither had left a will. One-half of the property went to the wife's heirs, who were a son and daughter by a prior marriage, and the other half went to the husband's heirs, who were three sisters and a brother.

These rules do not apply if you provide otherwise in a will, living trust or other document. For instance, it is not uncommon in wills and living trusts to provide that a devisee must survive you by some time longer than five days. A sample provision and its purpose are discussed in chapter 8 (page 105). There could be agreements among joint tenants or provisions in life insurance policies that similarly alter the usual rule of survivorship.

B.   Slayers

Another law deals with the situation in which a person who is to receive property from another person, whether by will, survivorship, or otherwise, kills the other person. The law states that the person doing the killing, called the slayer, does not receive the property. The law accomplishes this result by treating the slayer as if he or she had predeceased the person killed, called the decedent, even though the slayer survives the decedent.

For the law to apply, the slayer must take, or procure the taking of, the life of the decedent "with felonious intent." This can be established either by a conviction of such crimes as murder or manslaughter or by other evidence that such killing was "felonious and intentional." It might be possible, for instance, for a person to be acquitted and found not guilty of murder or manslaughter, but nevertheless be found by the probate court to have feloniously and intentionally killed the decedent. The underlying premise, of course, is that a person should not profit from his or her own wrongdoing.

The application of this law to specific types of property is as follows:

1. Probate Property

Any property that the slayer would have received as an heir (if there is no will), or as a devisee (if there is a will), is treated as if the slayer had predeceased the decedent.

2. Joint and Survivorship Property

The slayer receives an undivided one-half interest in the property for the rest of his or her life. The heirs or devisees of the decedent other than the slayer receive the balance of the interest in the property. For example, suppose the decedent and the slayer own rental property together. Under the rule, the slayer will receive half of the rental income for the rest of his or her life, but will have no interest in the property at the time of his or her death. If the slayer had survived, but not killed, the decedent, the slayer would have been entitled to all the income for life and could have given it away in a will at the time of death.

3. Life Estates and Remainders

If the slayer owns a remainder interest and the decedent was the life tenant, the life estate passes on to the decedent's heirs or devisees for a period of time equal to the normal life expectancy of the decedent, after which title will vest solely in the slayer.

4. Life Insurance

If the slayer is the primary beneficiary of a policy on the life of the decedent, the proceeds go to the secondary beneficiary or, if there is none, the proceeds are distributed as part of the decedent's estate.

C. Disclaimers

Another law that changes the usual rule of survivorship deals with a person's right not to have property forced on him or her. Although it may seem odd for a person to refuse to accept property that is either left under a will or trust or given as a lifetime gift, there may be several good reasons for doing so. Such a refusal to accept property is called a disclaimer.

First, you may discover that because of a change in circumstances, poor planning, or simply a desire not to be involved with a disfavored relative who is also receiving an interest in the same property, you would like to disclaim (or, as it is sometimes called, renounce) all your interest in the property. For instance, suppose a grandfather left a house with a life estate to your father, from whom you have been estranged for years, and the remainder to you. It might be easier for you to disclaim your remainder interest in that property rather than to confront your father about what to do with the house. Or you learn that the property is contaminated with hazardous waste.

A second reason might be that you already have a large estate, do not need more property, and are concerned about estate taxes. For instance, suppose your father dies leaving you securities worth

$500,000. His will provides that if you predecease him, your interest will be distributed to your children. You have an estate worth $1 million. If you accept the inheritance, your estate will be worth $1.5 million, which means that your estate could be subject to estate tax at your death. If you disclaim your interest, then for purposes of your father's will, you will be deemed to have predeceased him, and your $500,000 inheritance will be distributed to your children. For federal gift tax purposes, your father is deemed to have willed your share of his estate directly to your children, you are not treated as having made a gift to your children, and the inheritance does not become a part of your estate for estate tax purposes.

Or suppose, as a third reason, that you are having financial problems and are fighting off creditors. If you receive an inheritance, it might be reached by your creditors. By disclaiming your inheritance (and having it possibly go to another close family member), you can prevent your creditors from reaching the inheritance.

If you follow the required steps to make a disclaimer, you will be deemed to have predeceased the person who left you the property, and the property will be distributed to the contingent beneficiaries.

If you are entitled to receive property that is subject to a disclaimer and die or become incapacitated before you can effect a disclaimer, your personal representative, trustee, agent acting under a power of attorney or similar fiduciary can do it for you. You can disclaim less than all the property to which you are entitled.

The disclaimer must be in writing or retrievable electronic medium, describe the interest being disclaimed, be signed, and be delivered to the personal representative, trustee or other appropriate person. It may have to be filed with a court. It becomes irrevocable upon delivery, after which time you cannot change your mind and receive the property.

Under Oregon law, there is no statutory time limit by which you must make a disclaimer. Under federal law, however, for a disclaimer to be 'qualified' or valid for gift tax purposes, it must be made within nine months after the triggering event. For instance, if you are entitled to receive property under a will, you must disclaim within nine months after the testator's death.

You are barred from making a disclaimer if you accept the interest sought to be disclaimed, for instance by receiving interest, dividends, rent or other income from the property interest, if you voluntarily transfer or pledge the interest, or contract to do so, or if the interest sought to be disclaimed is sold pursuant to a judicial sale.

Here are some examples of interests which can be disclaimed:

(a) a devisee's or heir's interest in probate property, either under a will or when a person dies intestate;

(b) a 'future interest,' such as a remainder interest following the death of a life tenant, or a remainder beneficiary's interest under a trust following the death of the income beneficiary;

(c) a beneficiary's interest in a life insurance policy, annuity, IRA or other retirement account, or in a POD (payable on death) or TOD (transferable on death) account at a financial institution;

(d) a surviving joint tenant's interest in property owned jointly with right of survivorship.

Chapter 10

Marriage and Wills

A. Property Rights of Spouses

Many married couples place most or all of their property in joint and survivorship ownership. This is usually done as a matter of convenience and to avoid probate on the death of the first spouse. Other couples keep some or all of their properties in separate ownership. In large estates, separate ownership between spouses will open up estate tax savings possibilities.

1. Divorce

When it comes time to divide up the property in a divorce, the court will settle the property division if the couple cannot work out its own agreement. The law assumes that both spouses have contributed equally to the acquisition of property during the marriage, whether or not it is jointly or separately owned.

In addition to an equitable share of the marital assets, a spouse may be entitled to support or alimony from the other spouse. This support might be temporary or permanent depending on the respective earning abilities and other financial factors of the two spouses.

2. Death

All property owned by spouses jointly with right of survivorship automatically passes to the surviving spouse upon the first spouse's death. Probate property will be distributed to the surviving spouse only if the will so provides. If the deceased spouse leaves no will, the surviving spouse will receive his or her statutory share as heir.

A surviving spouse has the following rights in the probate property of a deceased spouse:

(a) the right to continue to occupy the family home and to receive support during probate;

(b) the right to act as personal representative;

(c) the right to inherit one-half of the probate property if there is no will and no surviving children of a prior marriage, or all the probate property if there are no issue or issue only of the present marriage;

(d) the right to elect against the will and take a share of the probate property. A surviving spouse's elective share is discussed in chapter 14 (page 174).

These laws govern probate property only. If the deceased spouse dies without probate property, the surviving spouse will have no property against which his or her rights can be asserted.

A spouse cannot give away property that is jointly owned and that requires signatures of both spouses. But there is no rule in Oregon that can stop a spouse from giving away his or her probate property during his lifetime, even if the intent is to deprive the other spouse of the property at death or dissolution of marriage.

In one case, Walter, who was married to Dorothy, deeded a parcel of real property in his own name to his mother and stepfather, so that they each owned an undivided one-third interest as tenants in common with Walter. Walter died intestate and his one-third interest passed to Dorothy. Dorothy sued Walter's mother and stepfather claiming that the conveyance was void as an intent by Walter to defeat her rights as his wife. The court ruled against Dorothy, holding that the mere fact that Walter intended to deprive her of the property was not sufficient grounds to set aside the deed.

B.   Marital Property Agreements

Agreements between spouses can waive the interests granted by law in each other's property either in divorce or at death. They can also grant greater rights to each other than the minimum granted by law. These agreements can be made prior to and in contemplation of marriage or during marriage. Both types of agreements are enforceable provided that they are in writing and entered into validly.

1. Premarital Agreements

Premarital agreements, also called prenuptial agreements, are carefully scrutinized by the courts because engaged couples frequently do not know much about each other's property and the agreements are often the consequence of emotion rather than logic. They are often challenged at the time of divorce or death of one of the spouses.

Oregon courts have ruled that when parties are engaged to be married, there exists a relationship of trust requiring good faith and full and frank disclosure of all assets. A valid premarital agreement must meet the following conditions:

(a) The parties must sign the agreement voluntarily. It should not be done in haste, but should be done long enough before the wedding to enable both parties to have time to examine and understand the agreement. An agreement would not be voluntary if on the way to the church, one party says to the other, "here, sign this agreement or I won't marry you."

(b) The agreement cannot be unfair to one party unless that party had full disclosure of the other party's property and financial obligations or waived the right to such disclosure. The purpose of this requirement is to avoid overreaching, concealment of assets, or sharp dealing by one party. Each party should attach to the agreement a complete list of property each party owns, with estimated values, amount of annual income, and a list of all long-term obligations.

(c) Each party should be represented by his and her own attorney. If one party refuses to retain a separate attorney, the agreement may still be valid, provided the party was offered the opportunity to consult with an attorney and declined to do so, and the agreement is fair and voluntarily entered into.

2. Postnuptial Agreements

Postnuptial agreements do not require the same precautions since presumably the spouses are familiar with each other's property. Nevertheless, the same precautions should be followed before signing the agreement.

3. Different Kinds of agreements

Marital property agreements can take many forms, but they generally fall into two main categories.

The first kind contemplates that each party will keep his or her assets in separate ownership. Typically, these agreements provide that each party releases all claims against the other's property in case of divorce or death. Each spouse is free to dispose of, manage, or otherwise deal with any separate property including the right to dispose by will. A provision that no alimony be paid will usually be enforced only where each spouse has sufficient assets of his or her own to remain self-supporting in case of divorce.

The second type of agreement assumes that the parties have commingled all their marital assets and own everything in joint and survivorship ownership. The planning is a little more complicated if it is a second marriage and each spouse wants to protect the children of a first marriage. Since all the property is owned jointly, there will be no probate on the first death. Typically the wills provide that upon the second death, half the property will be distributed to the children of the spouse first to die, and half to the children of the spouse second to die. To protect the children of the spouse first to die, such an agreement must have the following provisions:

(a) Each spouse agrees to sign a will containing agreed upon terms;

(b) During the joint lives of the spouses, both agree to neither amend nor revoke their wills without the consent of the other;

(c) After the death of the spouse first to die, the will of the surviving spouse will become irrevocable;

(d) If for any reason the survivor's will is revoked (e.g., upon the remarriage of the surviving spouse), the surviving spouse agrees to sign a new will containing terms consistent with the agreement;

(e) Each spouse waives his or her claim to an elective share in the other spouse's solely-owned property, or a claim to support or any other legal claim;

(f) After the death of the spouse first to die, the surviving spouse agrees not to give away or otherwise transfer any assets without adequate consideration. This is to minimize the risk that after the death of the spouse first to die, the surviving spouse gives away all the property and defeats the interests of the children of the deceased spouse; and,

(g) The contract can also cover the manner in which the spouses use the property during their joint lives, and may deal separately with the manner and treatment of the wife's own property, the husband's own property, and the jointly-owned assets, if any.

Although this form of agreement avoids probate on the death of the first spouse, it creates two other problems. The agreement may disqualify the property for the federal estate tax marital deduction on the death of the first spouse. It also severely restricts the freedom and flexibility of the surviving spouse to manage and use the marital property. In effect, the children of the deceased spouse will always be looking over the shoulder of the surviving spouse to make certain that the children's expectancy is not being mismanaged.

An alternative to this arrangement is to require that when the first spouse dies, the surviving spouse place half of the marital assets in an irrevocable trust for the children of the deceased spouse. The surviving spouse would have the right to income and could even be the trustee. The surviving spouse would be free to deal with the other half of the marital assets as desired.

C. Agreements for Unmarried Couples

A 1978 court decision established the basis for dealing with the breakup of relationships of unmarried couples. The court established the rule that property is to be distributed on the basis of the express or implied intent of the couple. If there is no written agreement, then the court is required to look at the particular circumstances of the couple.

Cohabitation, joint bank accounts, joint purchases, and shared income would all be evidence of an intent to pool resources for common benefit during the relationship. This would warrant an approximately equal division of the assets of the couple, regardless of whose name they were in.

If the court cannot find a general intent to share all the property that the couple accumulated during the relationship, it will review the intent and award each item of property separately. In one case, the court concluded that the couple intended to share the household items equally, but separately maintain large purchases, like the car, home, and motorcycle.

There is a great need for a written agreement between unmarried partners. If the relationship ends, the couple is not usually in agreement about the division of property. Unlike the dissolution of a marriage, there are no rules requiring an equitable division of property. There are also no rules regarding alimony or other support payments.

Absence of a written agreement creates even more of a problem for an unmarried couple upon the death of one of the parties. This is particularly true if the deceased party owned all or most of the property accumulated during the relationship in his or her own name and failed to make a will leaving such property to the surviving party. In this situation, the survivor may receive nothing from the deceased partner's estate.

D. Are You Really Married?

In view of the stark difference between the legal rights and duties of married and unmarried couples, it should not be too surprising that disputes arise over whether a couple is lawfully married, particularly after one or both of them have died.

Oregon requires a *ceremonial* marriage and does not recognize a so-called *common-law* marriage. Common-law marriages are recognized in some states, such as Idaho. Typically, such states require that the couple agree to be husband and wife, hold themselves out as husband and wife, and cohabit and otherwise mutually assume marital rights, duties, and obligations. No ceremony is required to validate a common-law marriage in those states that recognize it.

For a marriage made in Oregon to be valid, it must be solemnized. At least three days before the ceremony, the couple must obtain a marriage license issued by a county clerk. Then they must have their marriage solemnized by assenting or declaring in the presence of a minister, county clerk, or judicial officer, and at least two witnesses that they take each other to be husband and wife. While Oregon law does not recognize a common-law marriage entered into in Oregon, it will recognize common-law marriages validly consummated in states that do recognize them.

Chapter 11

Gifts to Minors

If you want to make a gift to a minor, you should take certain precautionary steps to protect the gift for the minor. Gifts can be made during your lifetime, or at your death by a provision in your will or living trust.

A.   What Is a Minor

Oregon law defines the age of majority different ways for different purposes. However, for most purposes, a minor is any person who is NOT:

(a) 18 years of age or older;

(b) married and 17 years of age or older; or

(c) 16 years of age or older and emancipated (this requires a special court hearing where the court concludes that the minor is mature enough to manage his or her own affairs without parental assistance).

B.   Minors and the Law

The law protects minors in two ways. First, the law says a minor can avoid transactions entered into while a minor. Second, the law provides that parents and certain other persons have authority to manage a minor's affairs.

If you make a gift to a minor, it will be difficult for anyone to purchase the property or otherwise contract with the minor. A minor may disaffirm any acquisition or sale of property or any contract made while a minor, either during minority or within a reasonable time after reaching majority.

This rule protects the minor, but it also makes it difficult for the minor to deal with property. If the property requires management, the court will appoint an adult or a trust company to manage it until the minor reaches majority.

There are some exceptions to the rule that minors may not contract. With each of these exceptions, the minor may not later disaffirm the minor's obligation to pay. For instance:

(a) A minor of any age may consent to treatment for venereal disease without parental consent.

(b) A minor 15 years of age or older may obtain medical or dental treatment without parental consent.

(c) A minor 16 years of age or older may donate blood without parental consent.

(d) A minor 14 years of age or older may obtain treatment for mental or emotional disorders or chemical dependency without parental approval.

(e) A minor 16 or 17 years of age, and a minor under 16 who is a parent of a child living with the minor or is pregnant may rent a residential unit and contract for utility services to that unit.

C. Custodianships

One of the best ways to make a small gift to a minor is through a custodianship. Under Oregon's law on gifts to minors, the Uniform Transfers to Minors Act, you can use a custodianship for present or future gifts of any kind of property, real or personal. All states have adopted some version of this uniform law.

1. How to Set Up a Custodianship

You can establish a custodianship by a lifetime transfer. For instance, you can open a savings account or purchase a mutual fund in the name of a custodian.

You can also name a custodian to receive property at your death. For instance, you can name a custodian in your will or living trust or as beneficiary of a life insurance policy.

A transfer to a custodian is irrevocable, whether made during your lifetime or at death, and conveys to and vests title and ownership of the property in the minor. In effect, the custodian holds and manages the minor's property for the minor until the minor reaches the distribution age and receives possession of the property.

There are two ways to establish a custodianship. If you want the custodianship to end and the minor to receive the custodial property at age 21, use the phrase: "as custodian for _____ (name of minor) under the Oregon Uniform Transfers to Minors Act."

You can also provide for a delayed transfer to the minor at an age you specify between 21 and 25. For this type of transfer, use the phrase: "as custodian for _____ (name of minor) under the Oregon Uniform Transfers to Minors Act until the minor attains the age of ____ years."

By using one of these simple phrases, you set up and adopt a statutory structure, similar to a detailed trust agreement, for managing and protecting a minor's property.

2. Who Can Be a Custodian?

Any adult, including the transferor, can be a custodian. The custodian can be, but need not be, a parent or other relative of the minor. A trust company can be a custodian, but will seldom be a practical choice. Custodianships should generally be used for relatively small gifts (whatever amount you are willing to turn over to the minor at age 25 or earlier) and most trust companies will not act as a custodian unless the value of the property is $100,000 or more.

If federal estate taxes are a concern for the transferor (generally, if the transferor's estate is worth more than $1 million; see chapter 16), the transferor should not act as custodian. If the transferor acts as custodian and then dies before the minor receives the property, the value of the property will be included in the transferor's estate for estate tax purposes.

3. Duties and Powers of the Custodian

A custodian may deliver or pay to the minor or expend for the minor's benefit as much of the custodial property as the custodian considers advisable for the minor's use and benefit, or the custodian may accumulate the income and wait to distribute all the income and principal to the minor at the distribution age. In exercising this discretion, the custodian may disregard the duty or ability of a parent to support the child or the fact that there may be other income or property available to the minor.

A custodian has the duty to:

(a) take control, collect, hold, manage, invest, and reinvest the property

(b) keep the property separate from all other property

(c) keep records of all transactions, including information necessary for the preparation of the minor's tax returns.

A custodian has all the powers necessary to carry out these duties.

4. Court Supervision

No court regularly monitors a custodianship. On rare occasions, court intervention may occur if the minor, or someone on the minor's behalf, petitions the court because:

(a) the custodian fails to use the custodial property for the minor's benefit,

(b) the custodian should be removed for cause or required to file a bond; or

(c) the minor wants an accounting.

5. Expenses and Compensation

The costs of a custodianship should be nominal. It can be set up with little or no help from an attorney, and there are no court costs or bond premiums. A custodian is entitled to reimbursement for reasonable expenses and, if the custodian is a person other than the transferor, reasonable compensation.

6. Ending the Custodianship

In most cases, a custodianship ends and the custodian must turn over the property when the minor reaches an age specified by the transferor (from 21 to 25). If the minor dies before the specified age, the custodian must transfer the property to the minor's estate, which will go to the minor's parents in most cases.

In two cases, the custodian must transfer the property to the minor at age 18. First, if you leave property to a minor in a will or trust and do not provide for a custodianship, a personal representative, trustee, or conservator can transfer property worth up to $30,000 (or more if a court approves) to a custodian. Second, if someone owes a minor money or holds property of a minor worth up to $5,000, that person can transfer the money or property to a custodian. In either case, the minor is entitled to the property at age 18.

7. Income and Gift Taxes

Because custodial property belongs to the minor, any income earned from the property is taxed to the minor, regardless of whether the custodian spends it for the minor or accumulates it. The minor's Social Security Number should be used as the taxpayer identification number for the custodial account. Income tax returns will have to be filed for the minor if the minor's unearned income from all sources, including income on custodial accounts, exceeds an inflation-adjusted amount, which for 2002 is $750.

If, however, the income is used to satisfy a parent's obligation of support (e.g., if the custodian buys food or clothing for the minor), then the income will be taxed to the parent.

If the unearned income of a minor under the age of 14, including income earned on custodial property, exceeds an inflation-adjusted amount (for 2002 it is $1500), the excess will be taxed at the highest marginal tax rate of the minor's parents. This tax is known as the 'Kiddie tax.' A parent can elect to report the child's excess income on the parent's own returns, in which event no returns will have to be filed for the child.

A lifetime transfer to a custodian qualifies as a gift to the minor for the federal gift tax annual exclusion if the minor receives the custodial property at age 21. If you specify an age other than 21 (that is, 22 to 25) as the distribution age, then transfers to the custodian do not qualify for the exclusion. The exclusion is $11,000 for transfers made in 2002 and is indexed for inflation (see chapter 17).

8. Custodian Account and Education

Custodial accounts may not be the best way to fund a minor's college education if the minor intends to apply for financial aid. In determining family assets available to pay educational expenses, colleges generally consider a higher percentage of the child's assets available than the parent's assets.

D. Conservatorships for Minors

A conservatorship is a court-supervised procedure for managing and protecting the property of either a minor or an incapacitated adult. (See chapter 12 for conservatorships for adults.) A conservator is the person or financial institution appointed by the court to handle the minor's property.

A conservatorship is different from a guardianship, which is the procedure for determining custody and ensuring the proper care of a minor. However, the same person can be both guardian and conservator.

1. How to Set Up a Conservatorship

A conservatorship is established by court order upon petition by an interested party. The court must determine that the minor owns money or property that requires management or protection. It would be unusual to make a lifetime gift to a minor with the intent that a conservator be appointed to manage the property.

A petition must be filed with a probate court naming the minor and the proposed conservator and giving information about the minor's property and family. A notice of petition must be given to the minor if the minor is 14 years of age or older, to the minor's parents, guardian, or custodian, and to other interested persons.

If no objections are filed, then the court appoints the conservator and sets the amount of the bond. The conservator must file an inventory of the property within 90 days after appointment.

2. Who Can Be a Conservator?

Any trust company, or any individual who is not incapacitated, financially incapable, a minor, or the minor's health care provider may act as a conservator. Two or more individuals may act as co-conservators.

The court will appoint the most suitable person who is willing to serve after giving consideration to the specific circumstances of the minor, any stated desire by the minor, any preference expressed by a parent of the minor, the minor's estate or property, and any impact on ease of administration that may result from the appointment.

3. Duties and Powers of a Conservator

A conservator must use the minor's property for the minor's care, support, education, or benefit. In determining standards for such payments, the conservator may consider the recommendations of the minor's parents or guardian unless the conservator knows that the parent or guardian is deriving personal financial benefit from such payments, including relief from any personal duty to support. This is different from the duty of a custodian, who may ignore any duty of support in making payments for a minor.

A conservator must also consider the size of the estate, the minor's accustomed standard of living, and other funds or sources available for the minor's support. Again, this is different from the duty of a custodian, who may ignore other funds available to the minor.

A conservator generally has all the powers necessary to manage the minor's property and to carry out the conservator's duties. He or she has all the powers of a trustee and of a guardian for the minor if none has been appointed

4. Court Supervision

A conservator must file an accounting with the court each year within 30 days of the anniversary of the conservator's appointment. He or she must also provide a copy of the accounting to the guardian and to the minor (if the minor is 14 years or older and capable of understanding it). The accounting must contain a list of all receipts and disbursements made during the year, a summary of any purchases or sales of property, and any other significant events that occurred during the year concerning the minor's financial affairs.

A conservator must file a surety bond equal to the value of the minor's property plus one year's income. It may be for a lower amount if the court orders that certain property is to be frozen, or if the court bars the conservator from selling.

A conservator has the same duties as a trustee and is subject to the same penalties for breach of those duties.

5. Expenses

There can be substantial costs in setting up and managing a conservatorship. The services of an attorney are required to establish the conservatorship, to prepare the inventory and annual accounting, and to advise the conservator on various matters. Court costs and bond premiums must also be paid. A conservator is entitled to reasonable compensation and expenses. All expenses, upon approval by the court, can be paid out of the minor's property.

6. Ending a Conservatorship

A conservatorship is terminated either when the minor becomes an adult or upon the minor's death, whichever comes first. A minor is defined in the conservatorship statute as any person who has not attained 18 years of age.

A conservatorship may be terminated early if the property consists solely of personal property worth less than $10,000. In that case, it can be distributed to a responsible adult for the minor's benefit.

7. Incapacity

If a minor is incapable of handling his or her own affairs when the age of majority is attained, then the conservatorship may be continued for the period of the incapacity. The incapacity must be established to the court's satisfaction.

8. Multiple Conservatorships

If two or more minors are children of a common parent, their conservatorships may be consolidated into one. Each minor's assets, however, must be segregated and separately managed.

E. Trusts

Trusts have the advantage of being flexible enough that you can tailor them precisely to your particular concerns or goals. For example, you can set up an irrevocable living trust for a minor to provide for the minor's education. For example, you can set up an irrevocable living trust for a minor to provide for the minor's education and have the income taxed to the minor or the trust rather than to you.

1. How to Set Up a Trust for a Minor

A trust is a contract between you and the trustees. A living trust is drafted and signed by you and the trustee, after which you fund the trust by transferring title to certain property. A testamentary trust is set out in your will or living trust and funded after your death when your personal representative or trustee of your living trust transfers the property to the trustee of the minor's trust.

2. Who Can Be a Trustee?

Any individual or trust company can act as trustee. There are no requirements that an individual must meet to qualify, except those that you set out in the trust document.

3. Duties and Powers

The primary duty of the trustee is to carry out the wishes set out in your trust document. For example, you can direct the trustee to make distributions of income to the minor for support only.

Under the Uniform Trustees' Powers Act, which is automatically part of your trust unless you direct otherwise, a trustee has all the powers necessary to carry out a trustee's duties, including power to invest and reinvest in accordance with Oregon's prudent investor law. However, you can limit the trustee's powers by specifying what kinds of investments the trustee can make.

4. No Court Supervision

A trustee must provide an annual accounting to the minor on request. There is no court supervision unless the minor or someone on the minor's behalf petitions the court to review the trustee's action. The trustee is required to post a bond only if the trust document requires it.

5. Expenses

Normally, the trust document provides for reasonable compensation and expenses for the trustee. However, you may set out a specific compensation formula. The other major costs are attorney fees for setting up the trust and any advice the attorney may provide.

6. Ending a Trust

The termination of a trust is up to you. For example, if you are setting up a trust to fund a college education, you may want it to continue it until the minor is at least 25 years old. If the property is of substantial value, you may want to continue it even longer.

7. Incapacity

You can provide that if the minor is incapacitated at the scheduled age for distribution, the trustee can continue the trust so long as such incapacity continues, including, if necessary, for the rest of the minor's life.

8. Multiple Trusts or Beneficiaries

You may direct that a single trust be set up for more than one minor. This is called a 'spray' or 'sprinkling' trust because the trustee is authorized to spray or sprinkle funds among the beneficiaries based on their separate medical, educational, or other needs. If one beneficiary has greater needs than another, then that beneficiary will receive greater benefits from the trust. There is no duty in such a trust to treat each beneficiary equally. This is a good plan when you are not certain that the property in the trust will be sufficient to meet the needs of each beneficiary if there is equal distribution.

9. Tax-planning Trusts

It is possible to set up a trust for a minor during your lifetime and have transfers to the trust qualify for the federal gift tax annual exclusion (currently $11,000 and indexed for inflation — see chapter 17).

One type of such trust is known as a Section 2503(c) trust (after the applicable Internal Revenue Code section). The trust must terminate when the minor reaches age 21. However, the trust can provide that the minor must make the election to terminate, and if the minor fails to do so at age 21, the trust can continue in effect until the minor reaches the age you specify, such as age 25.

The second type of trust is sometimes known as a Crummey trust (named after a court decision). Each year you transfer assets to the trust, you must give notice to the minor that you have transferred assets to the trust and that the minor has a limited time (typically 30 to 60 days) to withdraw the assets transferred. If the minor fails to withdraw the assets transferred, then they remain in the trust for the minor's benefit until the distribution age you specify.

F.   Guardianships

Chapter 8 discussed the importance of naming a guardian in your will for your minor children. This section describes the guardianship procedure in more detail.

1. Setting Up a Guardianship

A guardianship is established in the same way as a conservatorship, and frequently the same person is appointed both guardian and conservator.

A guardian is required to file a report with the court annually, within 30 days after each anniversary of appointment. In the report the guardian must give information about the minor, such as where the minor lives, the minor's physical and mental condition, and the guardian's activities during the year in taking care of the minor.

2. Who Can Be a Guardian?

To be appointed guardian, a person must have the same qualifications as a conservator.

3. Duties of a Guardian

A guardian has the powers and responsibilities of a parent who has the legal custody of a child, except that the guardian has no obligation to support the minor beyond the support that the guardian receives for the minor from other sources. The guardian is not liable for the acts of the minor. The guardian may consent to the marriage or adoption of the minor.

A guardian may receive money and personal property deliverable to the minor and apply money and property for the support, care, and education of the minor. The guardian must conserve any excess funds for the minor's needs. A guardian may not use the minor's funds for room and board furnished by the guardian or by the guardian's spouse, parent, or child without prior court approval.

G. Revocable Trust Accounts and POD Accounts for Minors

You can open up a bank account in your own name as trustee for a minor. Such arrangements are simple to set up, but are not necessarily good ways to make gifts to minors.

Since you are treated as the owner of the account until your death, all this arrangement will do is avoid probate of that account. Unless you have also put all your other property into nonprobate ownership, you will not avoid probate except with that account.

One possible advantage is that it does enable immediate distribution to the beneficiary upon the death of the trustee. However, these accounts frequently distort estate plans. For instance, if you want to give all your estate in equal shares to your children, but have one trust account for one child, then that child is going to receive what is in the trust account plus whatever you give that child under your will.

Financial institution employees are sometimes too casual in the way that they set up such accounts. Sometimes there are signature cards that set out your rights as trustee and when the minor is to receive the property. Other times, however, the account will simply state your name as trustee for the minor without any indication as to what happens at your death.

A typical bank card provides for a successor trustee if you die before the minor turns 18. However, if the successor trustee also dies before the minor reaches age 18, then it will be up to the bank to select a trustee. This leaves too much discretion in the management of your financial affairs to the bank.

If the minor dies before you do, then the funds come back into your estate as part of your probate property. If the minor dies before the successor trustee, then all the funds belong to the successor trustee.

There is no provision for the successor trustee's duties and powers, or for what happens if the minor is disabled at the age of 18, or has other problems.

When you die, if a successor trustee must act, then he or she can treat those funds as if they belong absolutely to him or her and not to the beneficiary, unless there is contrary language in the bank signature card.

In short, revocable trust accounts for minors should be used with great caution, only for small amounts of money, and then only after careful review and understanding of the bank signature card.

For the same reasons, you should also be cautious about naming minors as beneficiaries of POD accounts with financial institutions, and as TOD beneficiaries on stocks, bonds, and other securities.

If you decide to name a minor as beneficiary of a trust or POD account at a bank or a TOD beneficiary of a security, then provide that if the minor is under an age you specify (21 to 25) at your death, the beneficiary will be a custodian for the minor, under the Oregon Uniform Transfers to Minors Act.

H.   Funding a Minor's Education

There are a variety of ways to pay for a minor's current educational needs and to fund future education expenses. Each one has different tax and financial assistance consequences. Custodial accounts are one such technique. This section will describe other techniques.

1. Current Education Expenses

For minors presently in school, whether primary, secondary or post-secondary, parents have a duty of support to their children and incur no gift tax consequences in paying their educational expenses. However, a grandparent or other relative has no such duty and therefore should be aware of the possible gift tax consequences of such support.

For instance, if you are a grandparent and plan to help with a grandchild's education, you can pay each grandchild's tuition and other expenses. Payment of tuition directly to the school is excluded from federal gift tax and is not limited to $10,000 a year. You can also pay educational expenses other than tuition for each grandchild under the federal gift tax exclusion ($11,000 in 2002). If you are married, you and your spouse jointly can give up to twice the annual exclusion (or $22,000 in 2002) in educational expenses per grandchild per year.

2. Education Savings Accounts

Education savings accounts, sometimes called Section 529 plans, are a way to fund future post-secondary education expenses through a state agency. They are plans authorized by Congress and implemented by the states. Oregon and most other states now have such plans.

Plans vary from state to state, and many states do not require either the contributor or the beneficiary to be a resident, nor do they require the beneficiary to attend an in-state school. Investment options also vary from state to state and many people pick the state with the most attractive investment opportunities. Oregon requires the contributor or the beneficiary to be an Oregon resident, but does not require the beneficiary to attend an Oregon school.

You implement the plan by depositing funds into an account maintained by a state agency (in Oregon it is the Treasurer's office), and the state agency invests the funds for you. Most state agencies use a major mutual fund company to manage the investments.

Each state sets a limit on the amount which can be contributed to a plan for each minor; Oregon's is $250,000.

An education savings account is exempt from federal income taxation. The funds grow tax-deferred until the minor attends college. Distributions from the plan are also exempt from income tax to the extent that they are used to pay qualified education expenses. Earnings are also exempt from Oregon income taxation. In addition, Oregon permits an Oregon resident to deduct up to $2,000 annually for contributions to an Oregon education savings account.

You retain the right to change the beneficiary of the account. For instance, if you name one grandchild as a beneficiary and that grandchild does not go to college, you can name a different grandchild as beneficiary. If the new beneficiary is related to the former beneficiary, then the change in beneficiary, called a "roll-over distribution" is not subject to income taxation.

You may also withdraw the funds at any time. If you withdraw funds, then you must report the deferred income plus a 10% penalty on your own income tax returns.

Contributions to an educational savings account qualify for both the gift tax and the generation-skipping transfer tax annual exclusion ($11,000 in 2002 and indexed for inflation). You can transfer more than $11,000 in one year and have the gift qualify for the gift tax annual exclusion. This means that you can transfer $55,000 in one year and not use up any of your estate tax exemption ($1 million in 2002). A married couple can contribute $110,000 in one year for each grandchild or other beneficiary.

For financial assistance eligibility, funds in an educational savings account probably will not be considered owned by the beneficiary, and will therefore have less impact on financial assistance than a custodial account or an education IRA.

For more information about Oregon's plan, call toll-free at 866-772-8464 or visit its website at www.oregoncollegesavings.com.

3. Other Planning Tools

Coverdell Educational Savings accounts (formerly known as education IRAs) are similar to custodial accounts. You can deposit up to $2,000 in cash per year per grandchild or other beneficiary. You receive no deduction for the amount contributed.

The funds can grow income tax free and if they are used for educational purposes, the income is never taxed. One advantage over the education savings account is that the beneficiary can use the funds for primary and secondary as well as higher education expenses. Funds can be used for room and board as well as tuition.

No contributions can be made after the beneficiary's 18th birthday and the funds must be distributed to the beneficiary by age 30. You cannot make contributions to an account if your income exceeds certain limits.

Like custodial accounts, the funds in a Coverdell account are owned by the beneficiary and may lower the amount of the beneficiary's financial aid package.

Certain US savings bonds, including EE bonds issued after 1989 and Series I bonds, are not subject to income taxation if they are used for qualified higher education expenses, which includes tuition, but not room and board.

Chapter 12

Planning for Incapacity and End of Life

A. Health Care Decisions

In thinking about the possibility that you may become incapable of making decisions for yourself, whether because of illness, accident, or other reasons, you need to plan at two different levels. First, you need to decide who will make health care decisions for you and how those decisions will be made. Second, you should decide how and by whom your property and financial affairs will be managed.

B. Health Care Forms

Oregon has two health care forms, the advance directive and the declaration for mental health treatment. Both statutory forms became available in November 1993.

The advance directive is a form by which you can name representatives to make health care decisions for you if you become incapable of making them yourself. You can also direct how health care decisions will be made for you. See Sample #3.

The declaration for mental health treatment is a form of more limited scope. You can authorize certain types of mental health treatment if you have a mental health crisis. A sample is not included in this book.

Both new forms are available at hospitals, doctor's offices, through various health care and mental health organizations, and from attorneys. They can also be purchased at stores that sell legal forms.

1. The Advance Directive

The advance directive has two main parts: Part B, in which you can name one or two persons to make health care decisions for you, and Part C, in which you can give instructions on how health care decisions will be made for you. You may fill out Part B, Part C, or both. For instance, you may not have any persons you want to name as your health care representative, but may want to direct your health care providers on how decisions will be made for you in case of your incapacity. In such cases, you would fill out Part C, but not Part B.

In Part C you can state whether or not you want tube feeding or other kinds of life support, such as a respirator, if you have any one of four critical conditions. These provisions would apply if you are close to death, or terminally ill; you are permanently unconscious or in a persistent vegetative state; you have an advanced progressive illness, such as Alzheimer's disease; or life support would cause extraordinary suffering.

You can also insert additional conditions or instructions in Part C. For instance, if you have a degenerative disease and know that there are certain treatments you would want and certain treatments you would not want if the disease worsened, you could state those instructions in this part. You can also direct that you want to be an anatomical donor after your death.

2. Signing the Advance Directive

You must use the specific form set out by law. The form must be limited to health care decisions and cannot contain instructions on how to manage your property and financial affairs in case you become incapacitated.

You must sign or acknowledge the form in the presence of two witnesses. If you complete both Part B and Part C, then you must sign the form twice, once at the end of Part B and a second time at the end of Part C. The witnesses must sign Part D. They must meet certain qualifications, which are listed at the end of Part D.

Sample #3
The Advance Directive

ADVANCE DIRECTIVE

YOU DO NOT HAVE TO FILL OUT AND SIGN THIS FORM

PART A: IMPORTANT INFORMATION ABOUT THIS ADVANCE DIRECTIVE

This is an important legal document. It can control critical decisions about your health care. Before signing, consider these important facts:

Facts About Part B (Appointing a Health Care Representative)

You have the right to name a person to direct your health care when you cannot do so. This person is called your "health care representative." You can do this by using Part B of this form. Your representative must accept on Part E of this form.

You can write in this document any restrictions you want on how your representative will make decisions for you. Your representative must follow your desires as stated in this document or otherwise made known. If your desires are unknown, your representative must try to act in your best interest. Your representative can resign at any time.

Facts About Part C (Giving Health Care Instructions)

You also have the right to give instructions for health care providers to follow if you become unable to direct your care. You can do this by using Part C of this form.

Facts About Completing This Form

This form is valid only if you sign it voluntarily and when you are of sound mind. If you do not want an advance directive, you do not have to sign this form.

Unless you have limited the duration of this advance directive, it will not expire. If you have set an expiration date, and you become unable to direct your health care before that date, this advance directive will not expire until you are able to make those decisions again.

You may revoke this document at any time. To do so, notify your representative and your health care provider of the revocation.

Despite this document, you have the right to decide your own health care as long as you are able to do so.

If there is anything in this document that you do not understand, ask a lawyer to explain it to you.

You may sign PART B, PART C, or both parts. You may cross out words that do not express your wishes or add words that better express your wishes. Witnesses must sign PART D.

Print your NAME, BIRTHDATE AND ADDRESS here:

_____

(Name)

_____

(Birthdate)

_____

_____

(Address)

Unless revoked or suspended, this advance directive will continue for:

INITIAL ONE:

_____ My entire life
_____ Other period (____Years)

PART B: APPOINTMENT OF HEALTH CARE REPRESENTATIVE

I appoint _____ as my health care representative. My representative's address is _____,
and telephone number is (___) _____.

I appoint _____ as my alternate health care representative. My alternate's address is

_____, and telephone
number is (___) _____.

I authorize my representative (or alternate) to direct my health care when I cannot do so.

NOTE: You may not appoint your doctor, an employee of your doctor, or an owner, operator or employee of your health care facility, unless that person is related to you by blood, marriage or adoption or that person was appointed before your admission into the health care facility.

1. Limits. Special Conditions or Instructions: _____

_____

_____

INITIAL IF THIS APPLIES:

_____ I have executed a Health Care Instruction or Directive to Physicians. My representative is to honor it.

2. Life Support. "Life support" refers to any medical means for maintaining life, including procedures, devices and medications. If you refuse life support, you will still get routine measures to keep you clean and comfortable.

INITIAL IF THIS APPLIES:

_____ My representative **MAY** decide about life support for me. (If you do not initial this space, then your representative **MAY NOT** decide about life support.)

3. Tube Feeding. One sort of life support is food and water supplied artificially by medical device, known as tube feeding.

INITIAL IF THIS APPLIES:

_____ My representative **MAY** decide about tube feeding for me. (If you do not initial this space, then your representative **MAY NOT** decide about tube feeding.)

_____

(Date)

SIGN HERE TO APPOINT A HEALTH CARE REPRESENTATIVE

_____

(Signature of person making appointment)

PART C: HEALTH CARE INSTRUCTIONS

NOTE: In filling out these instructions, keep the following in mind:

• The term "as my physician recommends" means that you want your physician to try life support if your physician believes it could be helpful and then discontinue it if it is not helping your health condition or symptoms.

• "Life support" and "tube feeding" are defined in Part B above.

• If you refuse tube feeding, you should understand that malnutrition, dehydration and death will probably result.

• You will get care for your comfort and cleanliness, no matter what choices you make.

• You may either give specific instructions by filling out Items 1 to 4 below, or you may use the general instruction provided by Item 5.

Here are my desires about my health care if my doctor and another knowledgeable doctor confirm that I am in a medical condition described below:

1. Close to Death. If I am close to death and life support would only postpone the moment of my death:

A. INITIAL ONE:

____ I want to receive tube feeding.

____ I want tube feeding only as my physician recommends.

____ I DO NOT WANT tube feeding.

B. INITIAL ONE:

____ I want any other life support that may apply.

____ I want life support only as my physician recommends.

____ I want NO life support.

2. Permanently Unconscious. If I am unconscious and it is very unlikely that I will ever become conscious again:

A. INITIAL ONE: B. INITIAL ONE:

____ I want to receive tube   ____ I want any other life support
feeding.   that may apply.

____ I want tube feeding only as   ____ I want life support only as my
my physician recommends.   physician recommends.

____ I DO NOT WANT tube   ____ I want NO life support.
feeding.

3. Advanced Progressive Illness. If I have a progressive illness that will be fatal and is in an advanced stage, and I am consistently and permanently unable to communicate by any means, swallow food and water safely, care for myself and recognize my family and other people, and it is very unlikely that my condition will substantially improve:

A. INITIAL ONE: B. INITIAL ONE:

____ I want to receive tube feeding.   ____ I want any other life support
                                         that may apply.

____ I want tube feeding only as   ____ I want life support only as my
my physician recommends.   physician recommends.

____ I DO NOT WANT tube ____ I want NO life support.
feeding.

4. Extraordinary Suffering. If life support would not help my medical condition and would make me suffer permanent and severe pain:

A. INITIAL ONE: B. INITIAL ONE:

____ I want to receive tube feeding.   ____ I want any other life support
                                         that may apply.

____ I want tube feeding only as   ____ I want life support only as my
my physician recommends.   physician recommends.

____ I DO NOT WANT tube ____ I want NO life support.
feeding.

5. General Instruction.

INITIAL IF THIS APPLIES:

____ I do not want my life to be prolonged by life support. I also do not want tube feeding as life support. I want my doctors to allow me to die naturally if my doctor and another knowledgeable doctor confirm I am in any of the medical conditions listed in Items 1 to 4 above.

6. Additional Conditions or Instructions: _____

_____

_____

(Insert description of what you want done.)

7. Other Documents. A "health care power of attorney" is any document you may have signed to appoint a representative to make health care decisions for you.

INITIAL ONE:

_____ I have previously signed a health care power of attorney. I want it to remain in effect unless I appointed a health care representative after signing the health care power of attorney.

_____ I have a health care power of attorney, and **I REVOKE IT.**

_____ I **DO NOT** have a health care power of attorney.

_____

(Date)

SIGN HERE TO GIVE INSTRUCTIONS

_____

(Signature)

PART D: DECLARATION OF WITNESSES

We declare that the person signing this advance directive:

(a) Is personally known to us or has provided proof of identity;

(b) Signed or acknowledged that person's signature on this advance directive in our presence;

(c) Appears to be of sound mind and not under duress, fraud or undue influence;

(d) Has not appointed either of us as health care representative or alternative representative; and

(e) Is not a patient for whom either of us is attending physician.

Witnessed By:

_____

(Signature of Witness/Date)   (Printed Name of Witness)

_____

(Signature of Witness/Date)   (Printed Name of Witness)

NOTE: One witness must not be a relative (by blood, marriage or adoption) of the person signing this advance directive. That witness must also not be entitled to any portion of the person's estate upon death. That witness must also not own, operate or be employed at a health care facility where the person is a patient or resident.

PART E: ACCEPTANCE BY HEALTH CARE REPRESENTATIVE

I accept this appointment and agree to serve as health care representative. I understand I must act consistently with the desire of the person I represent, as expressed in this advance directive or otherwise made known to me. If I do not know the desire of the person I represent, I have a duty to act in what I believe in good faith to be that person's best interest. I understand that this document allows me to decide about that person's health care only while that person cannot do so. I understand that the person who appointed me may revoke this appointment. If I learn that this document has been suspended or revoked, I will inform the person's current health care provider if known to me.

_____

(Signature of Health Care Representative)   (Date)

_____

(Printed name)

_____

(Signature of Alternate Health Care Representative)   (Date)

_____

(Printed name)

If you appoint health care representatives, their appointment is not effective until they date and sign the form in Part E. You should have them sign after you have signed the form. They need not be present when you sign, nor do they need to sign in the presence of your witnesses.

3. Distributing the Advance Directive

Once your advance directive is signed by you, your witnesses, and your representatives, you should make enough copies to give one copy each to your health care representatives, to your physician or physicians, and to any hospital where you have been a recent patient.

Your physicians and hospital are required to place and keep your advance directive in your medical records. You may also wish to give copies of the directives to family members or close friends who are not named as your representative, and to your attorney and clergy. You should keep the original directive.

4. The POLST Form

If you have a serious medical condition and do not want to be resuscitated if you stop breathing, consider signing a POLST (physician order for life-sustaining treatment) to supplement your advance directive. This is a form by which your physician issues medical orders to make sure that your wishes concerning emergency medical services and your wishes expressed in your advance directive are carried out. Contact your physician if you are interested in this form.

5. Making Decisions for You

Your health care representative cannot act for you until and unless you become incapable of making your own health care decisions. Your attending physician or a court must determine your incapacity. If you put specific conditions or instructions in the advance directive, then your representative must follow your directions. If you do not, then your representative must act in your best interest. If you do not name a health care representative, then your health care provider must follow your instructions.

6. Former Health Care Documents

The advance directive replaces two older forms, the power of attorney for health care and the directive to physicians. Those older forms, however, continue to be valid in Oregon. If you have signed either form, you may continue to rely on the form as an enforceable expression of your wishes concerning who will make health care decisions for you and how they will be made if you become incapacitated.

However, health care professionals recommend that you sign the advance directive, even if you have already signed the older forms. The advance directive is more flexible and comprehensive than the older forms and gives you the opportunity to express your wishes on a broader range of health care situations.

Although the directive to physicians is effective for your life, the power of attorney for health care has a term of seven years, and you have to renew it after that time if you want it to continue to be in effect. If you sign an advance directive, you can make it effective for the rest of your life.

7. Comparison to Death with Dignity Act

The law authorizing use of the advance directive is separate from Oregon's Death with Dignity Act, discussed below. Unlike the

Death with Dignity Act, the advance directive law does not permit an affirmative or deliberate act or omission to end life, other than to allow the natural process of dying. In addition, the advance directive becomes effective only if and when you are incapable of making health care decisions yourself. A request to end life under the Death with Dignity Act is effective only if the person making the request is competent.

8. Sample Form

For a sample advance directive and instructions on how to complete it, contact :

Oregon Health Decisions
812 SW 10th Avenue, #203
Portland, OR 97205
Tel: 1-503-241-0744 or
1-800-422-4805
Fax: 1-503-885-8758
E-Mail: ohd1@teleport.com

9. Mental Health Declaration

The declaration for mental health treatment enables a person with a history of mental health disorders to give advance directions on how that person wants certain mental health decisions to be made if the person becomes incapable of making them.

It deals with four types of mental health treatments: convulsive treatment, use of psychoactive medications, outpatient services and up to 17 days of in-patient care. A person cannot authorize these kinds of mental health treatments in an advance directive.

For a sample mental health declaration and instructions on how to complete it, contact:

Oregon Office of Mental Health Services
P. O. Box 14250
Salem, OR 97309-0740
Tel: 1-503-945-9700

10. Death with Dignity Act

Under the Oregon Death with Dignity Act, a capable adult who is suffering from a terminal illness and has voluntarily expressed a wish to die may request medication for the purpose of ending life. The act is called the humane death law by those who support it and physician-assisted suicide by those who oppose it.

A physician is authorized to write a lethal prescription for the person making the request, and the person must self-administer the medication. The person must be an Oregon resident.

A number of safeguards are designed to assure that the person making the request is terminally ill, capable and acting voluntarily. These include the following:

(a) The request for medication must be signed and dated by the patient and witnessed by two or more individuals, who must attest that the patient is capable, is acting voluntarily and is not being coerced into signing the request.

(b) The attending physician must make a determination that the patient has a terminal disease, is capable, and is acting voluntarily.

(c) The attending physician must provide information to the patient, such as the patient's diagnosis and prognosis, to ensure that the patient is making an informed decision.

(d) The attending physician must refer the patient to a consulting physician to confirm the diagnosis and that the patient is capable and acting voluntarily.

(e) The attending physician must refer the patient for counseling, if appropriate, suggest that the patient notify next of kin, and advise the patient of the patient's right to rescind the request.

(f) To receive a prescription for medication to end life, the patient must make both an oral and a written request, and then reiterate the request, to the attending physician not less than 15 days after making the initial oral request.

For more information on the Oregon Death With Dignity Act, contact the following organizations:

Compassion in Dying of Oregon
6312 SW Capitol Highway, #410
Portland, OR 97201
Tel: 503-525-1956
Fax: 503-228-9160
Web Site: www.compassionindying.org
(Supports the Act)

Physicians for Compassionate Care
Education Foundation
P.O. Box 6042
Portland, OR 97228
Tel: 503-533-8154
Fax: 503-533-0429
(Opposes the Act)

C. Property and Financial Decisions

There are several tools for handling your property and
financial affairs if you become incapacitated. Making sure these
tools are put into effect while you are still competent can minimize
risk of loss of your property and disruption of your business and
financial affairs if you become incapacitated.

1. Conservatorships and Guardianships

Conservatorships and guardianships for adults are court
supervised proceedings for managing and protecting the property
and financial affairs and for providing for the care of an adult if
needed. At a minimum, you should indicate in writing your choice
for guardian or conservator if you become incapacitated. This
should be someone you can trust with your financial affairs (for a
conservator) and with decisions concerning where you live and
what medical care you receive (for a guardian).

A conservatorship ensures maximum protection because of
the bond, annual accounts, and court supervision requirements.
However, it is also the most costly tool for planning for financial
incapacity. A conservatorship terminates at death and cannot,
therefore, be used to avoid probate.

A conservatorship will make your financial affairs a matter of public record. It is the only choice for a person needing protection if no advance planning has been done.

2. Power of Attorney

A power of attorney is a document that you sign authorizing someone else to act as your agent. You are called the "principal" and the person you appoint is called the "agent" or "attorney-in-fact."

A power of attorney may be either general or limited. A general power of attorney authorizes your agent to sign your name and deal with your property to the same extent that you would. It gives blanket authority to the agent to act on your behalf with respect to your property. General powers of attorney should be used with great caution.

A limited, or special, power of attorney limits the authority of your agent to act only in certain transactions. For example, you can authorize a trusted relative or friend to sign your name for you on your bank account, or to sell your house for you.

A power of attorney can be used as a planning tool for incapacity because Oregon law authorizes your agent to act if you become disabled or incompetent. This is called a "durable" power of attorney. In Oregon a power of attorney is automatically durable unless you specify that it is not. No special language has to appear in the power of attorney to make it durable.

A power of attorney is automatically revoked by your death and cannot be used to avoid probate. You can revoke it while you are alive by a written revocation. You must be mentally competent to make or revoke a power of attorney. If you become incompetent after signing a power of attorney, the agent becomes accountable to your conservator for all the agent's actions.

Generally, a power of attorney must be recorded only if it is to be used by your agent to transfer an interest in real property. It should be recorded in the county where the real property is located.

The major attraction of a power of attorney is the ease with which it may be signed. Forms are readily available at office supply stores. However, because a power of attorney is so easy to sign and use, it can also be misused. If you want to sign a power of attorney to plan for your possible incapacity, you should do so with the assistance of an attorney.

3. Revocable Living Trust

Chapters 4 and 5 described the funded revocable living trust. If you are considering this as a means of planning for incapacity, consider the following:

(a) A living trust is more expensive than a power of attorney to set up.

(b) A living trust can be tailored to your particular desires and needs regarding the management and distribution of your assets while you are incapacitated.

(c) A living trust can be used to avoid probate, so your financial affairs do not become public record at your death.

(d) A living trust is generally more effective and reliable than a power of attorney, which may not be accepted by financial institutions, stockbrokers, or title companies.

4. Joint Bank Accounts

Be cautious abut using a joint bank account to plan for incapacity.

A joint bank account is easy to set up, and for that reason it is easy to abuse. There is always the risk that the other joint owner may predecease you, in which case the account will be back in your own name. If you are already incapacitated, then a conservator may have to be appointed for you. Another risk is that the other joint owner may have tax, creditor, or domestic problems, in which case you may lose the funds in your joint account, or the account may end up in litigation.

Here are a few suggestions:

(a) Set up the account only with someone you trust. Your spouse of many years is a safe choice.

(b) If you want another person to have authority to sign on your account, but you do not want the account to go automatically to that person at your death, grant the person a limited power of attorney, but keep the account in your own name. Most banks have forms for this purpose. Use a joint and survivorship bank account only if you also want the person to have the funds in the account at your death.

(c) Sign a letter of understanding with the other joint owner setting out how and when the funds in the account are to be used.

A joint bank account is only a partial solution. You will still have to plan for the management of your other property if you become incapacitated.

D. Long-Term Health Care and Medicaid

A major concern for older persons today is the prospect that an extended stay in a nursing home may deplete their estates and leave them penniless. Long-term insurance is now available to cover such costs. In addition, with advance planning, a family can take steps to minimize financial impoverishment and conserve assets when a person must be in a nursing home for a long period. The primary means of conserving assets is to qualify for Medicaid without having to spend all the person's assets and thus impoverish the person first.

Medicaid is a combined federal-state medical assistance program which pays the nursing home costs for persons who are too poor to pay. It also covers other health care services, such as residential care facilities, adult foster care, in home care, physician services, prescription drugs, and medical transportation.

To qualify for Medicaid, a person must meet both an income and a resource test. To meet the income test, gross monthly income must be at or below 300% of the full SSI standard for a person living alone, an amount which periodically changes. SSI (Supplemental Security Income) is a federal benefit based on financial need for low or no-income persons who are blind, disabled or age 65 or older.

If your income exceeds the gross income limitation, then you face the risk of not being able to qualify for Medicaid yet not being able to afford the cost of a nursing home. One way to qualify is to sign a special form of irrevocable trust known as an "income-cap trust." Basically, you agree with the state that all of your income will be transferred to the trustee, to be distributed according to Medicaid priorities. The trustee will have authority to make distributions from the trust for your personal needs, administrative costs, family support obligations, nursing home, and other health care costs. Any funds remaining in the trust at your death must be turned over to the state.

To meet the resource, or asset test, you cannot own any "available" resources, other than excluded resources. If you are married, then your spouse's resources are considered available to you, even if the resources are in your spouse's name alone. A resource is considered available to you if you or your spouse have the right to sell or use it. Examples include bank and brokerage accounts, stocks and bonds, cash value life insurance, real property, motor vehicles, and retirement accounts.

The primary excluded resources are the following:

(a) cash up to $2,000;

(b) your home, provided you are residing in it or reasonably expect to return to it, or if your spouse, a minor or disabled child, or other dependent relative is residing in it;

(c) one automobile and all personal and household belongings;

(d) burial merchandise, such as a casket and vault or cemetery plot;

(e) a burial fund, prepaid burial insurance, or a life insurance policy with a death benefit of up to $1,500.

If you are married, then the spouse not applying for Medicaid, called the "community spouse," may retain some of your income and resources. The purpose of this provision is to prevent the community spouse from becoming impoverished.

Any resources that do not qualify as excluded resources, and, if you are married, any resources not allocated to the community spouse, must be spent or given away before you can qualify for Medicaid.

In order to preserve resources in excess of excluded resources and resources allocated to a community spouse, you have to transfer resources out of your name, typically to children. Giving away resources to qualify for Medicaid, however, requires long-term advance planning because of the ability of the state to look back and impose a transfer penalty by delaying your eligibility date for gifts made too soon before you apply for Medicaid. This rule does not apply to gifts between spouses.

When you apply for Medicaid, the state looks back and analyzes all gifts which you made during the 36 months prior to the date of your application. If you make a gift out of a trust, the look-back period is 60 months. Any gifts made before the applicable look-back period do not need to be reported.

If you make any gifts during the look-back period, then you may be ineligible for Medicaid for the number of months equal to the value of all gifts made divided by the average monthly cost of nursing home care in Oregon. Whether or not a gift within the look-back period makes you ineligible for a period of time depends on the value of the gift and the date of application.

In making gifts to children or other family members, you must take into account not only the Medicaid transfer penalty, but also the gift, estate and income tax consequences of such gifts, as well as your loss of control over the resources you give away.

E. Elder Abuse

Senior and disabled adults are particularly susceptible to abuse, ranging from physical abuse to neglect, abandonment and psychological abuse. Oregon law requires both public officials as well as private officials, such as physicians, lawyers and members of the clergy, to report abuse to the Senior and Disabled Services Division, which will investigate to determine the nature and cause of the abuse. In addition, lawsuits can be brought against the persons responsible for the abuse to restrain the abuse and to recover damages.

Chapter 13

Anatomical Gifts and Final Arrangements

One of the easiest ways to "work a miracle," as a brochure from the Oregon Donor Program puts it, and give the gift of life is to donate all or part of your body to medical science or for transplants. You can make this gift under the Uniform Anatomical Gifts Act, which is in effect in every state.

A. Who May Be a Donor?

There are three ways to make anatomical gifts. First, you can make a gift of all or part of your body, to take effect at your death, by completing a document of gift. To do so, you must be capable of making health care decisions and be 18 years of age or older.

Second, you can delegate authority to make an anatomical gift to any person 18 years of age or older. The delegation of authority must be in writing and signed by the donor. Third, if a family member has died, you can make an anatomical gift of all or part of the deceased family member's body. The deceased family member can be an adult or a minor, including a stillborn infant or fetus.

Persons who are authorized to donate a deceased person's body, in order of priority, are the deceased person's:

(a) spouse;

(b) child 18 years of age or older;

(c) parent (either one);

(d) brother or sister 18 years of age or older;

(e) guardian;

(f) next of kin;

(g) personal representative; or

(h) public health officer.

The family members listed may not make a gift if an individual in a prior class is available to make the gift, the individual proposing to make the gift knows of a refusal or contrary indication by the deceased person, or the individual proposing to make the gift knows of an objection by another member of the individual's class or a member of a prior class.

B.   How to Make the Gift

There are four ways to document your intent to become an anatomical donor. Because of the importance of knowing that you are a donor immediately at your death, you may wish to use more than one, and perhaps all four ways.

1. Sign a Donor Card

You can sign a donor card. Your signature need not be witnessed. However, if you cannot sign, the card must be signed by another individual and two witnesses, all of whom must sign at your direction and in your presence and in the presence of each other. Once you sign the card, you should carry it in your wallet.

You may get a donor card and other information about anatomical gifts from the Oregon Donor Program. It is a public education coalition of six organizations promoting anatomical gifts. Its address and telephone numbers are:

Oregon Donor Program
P.O. Box 532
Portland, Oregon 97207
1-800-452-1369 or 503-494-7888 in Portland
Web site: www.ordonorprogram.org

2. Sign a Form at the Motor Vehicle Division

You can sign a form at the Motor Vehicle Division, which will constitute a document of gift, and have your gift designated on your driver's license or identification card.

3. Make the Gift in Your Will

You can insert a provision in your will. If you do so, your anatomical gift is valid, even if your will is not admitted to probate or is declared invalid. However, a will may not be a practical way of making an anatomical gift, because your will may not be located and read until it is too late to carry out your wishes.

4. Make the Gift in Your Advance Directive

You can also make an anatomical gift in your advance directive. It is also a good idea to notify your family, clergy, doctor, and lawyer that you have made an anatomical gift. Make the gift in your advance directive and distribute copies to your family and professional advisors.

C. How to Amend or Revoke the Gift

You may amend or revoke an anatomical gift by the following means:

(a) a signed statement;

(b) an oral statement made in the presence of two individuals;

(c) any form of communication during a terminal illness, addressed to a physician or surgeon;

(d) in the case of a gift made by driver's license or identification card application, lapse of the license, cancellation of the card, or by a statement made and delivered in the manner specified by the Department of Transportation;

(e) destruction, cancellation, or mutilation of the document of gift in the case of a gift not made by driver's license or identification card; and

(f) in the case of a gift made by will, amendment or revocation of the will.

An anatomical gift which you do not revoke before death is irrevocable and does not require the concurrence or consent of a family member or any other person after your death.

D. Duties of Procurement Organization

An organization authorized to accept an anatomical gift is known as a "procurement organization." The six organizations which are members of the Oregon Donor Program are the principal procurement organizations in Oregon.

A procurement organization may either accept or reject an anatomical gift. If the gift is of the entire body, then the organization may allow embalming and use of the body in funeral services. If the gift is of a part of the body, the organization must cause the part to be removed without unnecessary mutilation.

If a person is in a hospital, is near death, and the person or the family has authorized an anatomical gift, then the hospital notifies the appropriate procurement organization. According to the Oregon Donor program, surgical removal of organs and tissues takes place either at a hospital or at a funeral home.

E. Final Arrangements

You will greatly relieve your family's distress at your death if you leave them an informal letter of instructions detailing your wishes on a funeral, whether you want cremation and where you will be buried. Prearranging your funeral and burial can also reduce your family's anxiety at the difficult time of your death.

If you are concerned about a possible dispute among family or friends on the disposition of your remains, you can leave a formal written and witnessed document directing how your remains will be disposed of, or you can prearrange your funeral and burial with a funeral home. If you use either option, your directions cannot be cancelled or substantially revised unless there are insufficient funds to pay for the disposition you have directed.

You can also appoint a person to be in charge of your funeral arrangements. If you do not, and if you do not give binding directions or prearrange your funeral, the persons who are authorized to make anatomical gifts for you, in the same order of priority, may direct the lawful disposition of your remains.

Chapter 14

Probate Administration

Probate administration, or simply probate, as it is sometimes called, is a court-supervised procedure for settling the estate of a deceased person (known as the decedent) who dies owning probate property. Administration is not necessary for nonprobate property. (This distinction is explained in chapter 1.)

The purpose of probate is to settle all claims against the estate, whether by creditors or by heirs, and to transfer title to the probate property to the devisees if the decedent left a will, or to the heirs if the decedent died without a will. Generally, probate is necessary unless the estate is very small or if the decedent had only certain types of probate property (see chapter 15).

An Oregon probate court will have jurisdiction to probate all personal property located in Oregon or elsewhere. It also has jurisdiction to probate real property in Oregon. If the decedent had real property outside Oregon, a second or ancillary probate may be required in the state where the real property is located. If the decedent was not a resident of Oregon, an Oregon probate court still has jurisdiction to probate any real property located in the state.

A. Locating the Will

The first step is to provide for funeral, burial, or other disposition of the body. Simultaneously, and equally as important, the family should ascertain whether the decedent left a will. The most likely places for storing a will are the family home, the offices of the decedent's attorney, a trust company, the decedent's safe deposit box, or the decedent's bank. It is important to locate the most recent will.

If the will is in the decedent's safe deposit box, the person named in the will as personal representative must follow the procedure described in chapter 7 to obtain the will.

Whoever has custody of a will must turn it over to the personal representative named in the will or the probate court within 30 days after receiving notice of the decedent's death.

There is no need to rush to the bank and try to close out the decedent's bank accounts before the state receives notice of the death. Oregon does not put a hold on or "freeze" bank accounts and safe deposit boxes when a person dies. If a bank account or safe deposit box is in the decedent's sole name, the personal representative can withdraw the funds in a bank account or remove the contents of a safe deposit box as soon as the probate court has appointed the personal representative. If a bank account or safe deposit box is owned jointly by the decedent and another person, the surviving joint owner can withdraw the funds or remove the contents immediately after the decedent's death.

B.   Who Handles the Probate?

The person in charge of the probate is called the personal representative. The personal representative will be one or more persons named in the will. If the person is named in the will, he or she is known as the executor (if male) or the executrix (if female). If there is no will, the court will appoint a qualified person or trust company. If there is no will, the person is called an administrator (if male) or an administratrix (if female).

The personal representative should retain an experienced probate attorney for assistance in administering the estate. Although the personal representative may, and often will, select the attorney who prepared the will, there is no legal requirement that this be done. The personal representative is free to select any attorney.

The personal representative and the attorney must decide on the division of functions between them. The attorney prepares and submits all documents that must be filed with the court. The personal representative, with the advice of the attorney, should locate and secure all property of the decedent, pay all claims, arrange for the sale of any property which is to be sold, communicate with beneficiaries, and arrange for final distribution to them. The more the personal representative can do, the less the attorney will have to do, and the less expensive administration should be.

The personal representative may also have to hire other professionals. An accountant may have to be retained for preparing income, estate, inheritance, and gift tax returns if the attorney does not do the tax work. The personal representative may also have to hire appraisers, real estate agents, stockbrokers, or estate sale professionals to sell assets of the estate.

C.   How to Start Probate Proceedings

Once it has been determined that probate administration is necessary, the next step is for the personal representative to file a petition for the court's approval of the appointment and, if there is a will, for its admission to probate.

A will must be proved. It may be proved by the affidavits of the attesting witnesses swearing that they saw the decedent sign the will, and, at the time, the decedent appeared to be of sound mind and over the age of 18 years. If the witnesses cannot be found and no affidavits were signed at the time the will was signed, then the will may be proved by testimony or other evidence of the genuineness of the decedent's signature or that of at least one of the witnesses.

When the original will cannot be found, proof may sometimes be made with a copy, if available, and by the affidavit or testimony of the will's drafter or witnesses.

More formal evidence of validity must be presented if the will is challenged.

D.   Personal Representative's Bond

A personal representative must file a surety bond with the court, unless:

(a) the will provides that no bond is required;

(b) the personal representative is the sole heir or devisee of the estate; or

(c) all heirs and devisees agree in writing that the bond may be waived.

The court may require a bond even if one or more of these conditions is met.

The purpose of the bond is to protect the beneficiaries and creditors of the estate from misconduct and mismanagement by the personal representative. The bond must be from a commercial surety company unless the court approves one or more personal sureties. The annual premium for a commercial surety bond is about $5 per $1,000 of assets, with a minimum premium of $100.

The amount of the bond is set by the court, which takes into account the nature of the assets, their current value, the amount of expected income, and the probable indebtedness and taxes. The bond cannot be less than $1,000. The amount of the bond can be reduced if the court "freezes" certain assets of the estate, that is, prohibits the personal representative from selling, transferring, or encumbering assets without further order of the court.

E.   Court Appointment of the Personal Representative

Once the court has appointed a personal representative and the bond, if necessary, has been filed, the court issues a document known as either Letters Testamentary (if a will has been admitted to probate) or Letters of Administration (where there is no will) certifying that the personal representative has been appointed. The personal representative then has authority to deal with the assets of the estate.

F.   Notice to Heirs and Devisees

Immediately after appointment, one of the first steps the personal representative must take is to send a required notice to all devisees and heirs. The notice together with a copy of the death certificate must be sent to the Estate Administration Unit of the Oregon Department of Human Resources.

The notice must inform each heir and devisee of the name of the court and file number, the decedent's name and date of death, whether or not the will has been admitted to probate, the name and address of the personal representative and the attorney, the date of the personal representative's appointment, a statement advising each devisee or heir that his or her rights may be affected by the proceeding, and information as to where additional information can be obtained.

The personal representative must also send the required notice to any person who the personal representative knows intends to contest the will, claim there is another will, or claim there was some agreement with the decedent concerning the will.

Proof of the notice must be filed with the probate court within thirty days after appointment.

There is no requirement for a formal reading of the will by the attorney. Many people think this is required because they see the will read on television shows and in movies. Although the will becomes a part of the probate court's record and is open to the public, the personal representative is not required to send a copy to the heirs and devisees. Normally, however, the personal representative either sends a copy of the will, or at least excerpts from it, to the heirs and devisees along with the required notice.

G.   Notifying Interested Persons

The personal representative must also immediately publish a notice in a newspaper of general circulation in the county where the probate proceeding is pending, known as "Notice to Interested Persons," informing creditors and other interested persons of the title of the court, the name of the decedent, the name and address of the personal representative where claims may be presented, and a statement requiring anyone having claims against the estate to present claims within four months after first publication. The notice must appear in the newspaper once in each of three consecutive weeks.

H. Listing the Property

Within 60 days after appointment, the personal representative must file an inventory, unless the court grants a longer time. The inventory must list all probate property of the decedent which has come into the personal representative's possession or knowledge, together with the personal representative's estimate of the true cash values of the assets as of the date of death.

Generally, the personal representative need not get accurate appraisals of all assets for purposes of probate administration. However, it may be necessary for the personal representative to get such appraisals for income and death tax purposes. If the personal representative seeks appraisals for those reasons, those values should also be used for the probate inventory.

I. What the Personal Representative Does

The general duties of the personal representative are to collect the income from property of the estate and to preserve, settle, and distribute the estate in accordance with the terms of the will, or in accordance with Oregon law if there is no will, as expeditiously and with as little sacrifice of value as is reasonable under the circum-stances.

Duties include collecting assets of the decedent, paying claims, administration expenses, death taxes, and income, gift or property taxes, preserving and protecting the assets during the course of administration, and then distributing the assets to the persons entitled to them.

Generally, the personal representative is expected to proceed with administration, settlement, and distribution of the estate without court order. The attorney should counsel and assist the personal representative in each stage and prepare papers for filing with the court.

The personal representative has the general powers to carry out these duties, including the power to sell, mortgage, lease, or otherwise deal with the property of the estate; to make investments of assets of the estate for limited purposes; to borrow money; to complete contracts of the decedent; and to continue any business venture in which the decedent was engaged at his or her death.

J.   Claims Against the Estate

The personal representative has an affirmative duty to identify and notify persons who may have claims against the estate. During the first three months following appointment, the personal representative must make a reasonably diligent effort to investigate the financial records and affairs of the decedent to ascertain the names and addresses of possible claimants. The personal representative can get an extension of time to complete this search. Within 30 days after the end of this search period, the personal representative must give notice to each identified claimant whose claim has not been presented, accepted or paid in full. If a personal representative fails to give this notice, and a person who should have been notified files a claim after distribution has been made, the personal representative and any person receiving assets which should have gone to the claimant (whether heir, devisee, or another claimant) will have to pay the omitted claimant out of their own assets.

Generally, however, the personal representative pays all claims as they are presented. A personal representative is not required to pay any claim until after the lapse of the four-month waiting period, and should not do so if there is any question about the solvency of the estate. He or she does not usually worry about the formalities of formal claims. However, the personal representative can insist on following the proper procedures, especially if the claim may be disputed or if the estate is insolvent. In such event, the person making the claim must present a written claim to the personal representative describing the nature and amount of the claim, the names and addresses of the claimants, and the attorney, if any. The claim must be presented to the personal representative at the address given in the notice to interested persons.

A claim is barred from payment unless it is presented within four months after date of first publication of notice to interested persons, or if the personal representative was required to give notice to a claimant, within 30 days after such notice. However, a claimant whose claim is barred is still entitled to payment, provided that the claimant presents the claim before the final account is filed and before two years after the date of death, but only to the extent of assets available after payment of expenses and after payment of timely-filed claims. If a claimant does not receive actual notice of the probate, the claim must be paid if the claim is filed within two years after death and would have been allowed if timely presented.

Once a claim has been presented, it is considered allowed unless the personal representative mails or delivers notice of disallowance to the claimant and his or her attorney within 60 days after presentment. The disallowed claim is barred unless, within 30 days after mailing of the notice, the claimant either files a request for summary determination in the probate proceeding or begins a separate lawsuit against the personal representative.

If an estate is insolvent, the personal representative must make payment in the following order:

(a) support for spouse and children up to one-half of the value of the estate, with periodic payments to continue for not more than one year after death;

(b) the fees of the personal representative and the attorney and other expenses of administration;

(c) expenses of a "plain and decent" funeral and disposition of the remains;

(d) debts and taxes with preference under federal law;

(e) reasonable and necessary hospital and medical expenses of last illness;

(f) certain state taxes;

(g) wages due employees of the decedent earned within 90 days before death;

(h) child support arrearages;

(i) reimbursement for certain public assistance benefits; and

(j) all other claims.

K. What Happens when Probate Is Delayed?

A simple probate administration should be completed within a year after a petition for probate is filed. There can be many reasons for delays beyond a one-year period, such as lawsuits involving the estate, delays in obtaining necessary tax clearances, and the necessity of completing sales of assets to have enough cash to pay claims and taxes.

Sometimes it is better for the beneficiaries and for the estate to keep the estate open beyond one year, especially for income tax purposes. However, sometimes the reason is simply attorney procrastination. The beneficiaries are entitled to information on the status of the estate and when they can reasonably expect to receive distribution.

If there is going to be some delay in final distribution of all assets, it is possible to obtain a court order permitting a partial distribution. However, there must be sufficient assets left after distribution to pay support of the spouse and children, expenses of administration, and all unpaid claims.

If the estate is going to take longer than a year to probate, the personal representative must file an annual accounting within 30 days after the anniversary of his or her appointment reporting on the management of the estate.

L. Final Account

When the personal representative is ready to make final distribution of the estate, he or she must file a final account with the court. If the estate is probated in less than a year, this will be the only accounting that must be filed with the court. There are two forms of an accounting: a detailed final account and a short-form verified statement.

The verified statement is an expeditious way of closing an estate where all creditors have been paid in full and all heirs or devisees consent in writing to the short-form procedure.

All the verified statement must say is that all creditors have been paid in full and all Oregon income and personal property taxes have been paid. It must be accompanied by a petition signed by all the beneficiaries requesting the personal representative to distribute the property to the persons entitled to it as provided in the will, under the laws of intestate succession, or as agreed upon by the beneficiaries. It is not necessary to file any formal notice to the distributees nor is there any waiting period between the time for filing and the time for obtaining an order of distribution.

The formal final account requires a detailed accounting of all money and property received and all disbursements made, supported by canceled checks or other vouchers. It must also generally describe what the personal representative did during the course of administration. After the final account is filed, the personal representative must send a notice to each heir or devisee, and to any creditors who have not received payment in full. The notice states that the final account has been filed and that the interested persons have not less than 20 days to file an objection to the accounting.

If any objections are filed, the court hears the objections. If no objections are filed, or if a short form verified statement has been filed, then the court enters a decree of final distribution, which approves the personal representative's administration of the estate, fixes fees for the personal representative and the attorneys, and directs distribution of the remaining assets of the estate to persons entitled to them.

After the court enters its decree of final distribution, the personal representative then distributes the property in accordance with that decree, gets appropriate receipts, and files the receipts or other proof of distribution, sometimes with a supplemental final account, with the court. The court then enters an order discharging the personal representative and closing the estate.

M. Paying the Personal Representative and Attorneys

The personal representative is entitled to a fee set by statute. The amount is calculated as a percentage of the whole estate, which is the value of the inventory, plus all income earned or gains realized during administration. The percentages (assuming an estate of $10,000 or more) are:

(a) $10,000 to $50,000: $430 plus 3% of excess over $10,000;

(b) Over $50,000: $1,630 plus 2% of excess over $50,000.

The personal representative is also entitled to a fee equal to 1% of the nonprobate property (other than life insurance proceeds). In addition, if extraordinary services have been performed by the personal representative, such as filing a lawsuit to collect an asset, the personal representative may be entitled to a fee for extraordinary services.

The attorney for the personal representative is also entitled to a fee that is fixed by the court. This fee is based primarily on the number of hours spent by the attorney, but also on factors such as the attorney's experience, the skill displayed, the results obtained, and the amount of responsibility assumed by the attorney.

N. Rights of the Spouse and Dependent Children During Probate

Normally the family residence is owned jointly by husband and wife. In the unusual situation that it is not, and thus becomes a probate asset, the surviving spouse and any dependent children of the decedent may continue to occupy the residence for one year after death. They have an obligation to keep the family residence in repair, keep it adequately insured, and pay all taxes and liens as they become due. They must not permit any liens to attach to the property. If there is no surviving spouse, the dependent children still have the right to live in the family residence for one year after the death of the second parent. No court order is required.

A surviving spouse and dependent children are also entitled to support during probate. Support may be ordered upon appropriate petition to the court. To determine the amount of support, the court considers the estate's solvency, the property available for support, and the property inherited by or devised to the spouse and children.

The court can provide support by transferring title to real or personal property or by periodic payments of money. However, the periodic payments cannot continue for more than two years after death. If the support payments would render the estate insolvent, support cannot exceed one-half of the value of the estate, nor can periodic payments continue for more than one year after death. Support payments have priority over claims and expenses of administration and over any share for the distributees.

Finally, if it appears that reasonable provision for support of the spouse and minor children warrants that the whole estate (after payment of claims, taxes, and expenses of administration) be set apart for support, the court may do so four months after the notice to interested persons is published. The estate is then closed.

O. The Surviving Spouse's Minimum Share

Under Oregon's law of intestate succession, if you die without a will, your spouse is entitled to 50% of your probate property if there are children or other surviving issue who are not issue of your spouse, or the entire estate if there are no such surviving issue or only issue of your spouse. If you have a will, you may give your spouse less than the share of your estate to which he or she would be entitled without a will. However, you cannot totally disinherit your spouse. If you leave your spouse less than what he or she is entitled to, your spouse may elect to take the amount granted under Oregon law rather than what you left him or her in your will.

This "elective share" is equal to 25% of your probate property available for distribution. There is an additional limitation, however, requiring that nonprobate property be taken into account. This 25% will be reduced if the total of the elective share and nonprobate property received by your spouse exceeds 50% of the total probate and nonprobate property.

If the parties are not living together at the time of the death, the court has the discretion to deny the surviving spouse the right "to elect" against the will. In exercising its discretion, the court looks at such circumstances as the length of the marriage, whether it was a first or subsequent marriage for either or both spouses, the contribution of the surviving spouse to the property of the decedent in the form of services or transfer of property, and the length and cause of separation.

To elect against the will, a surviving spouse must file a statement with the probate court that he or she elects to take the elective share. The statement must be filed within 90 days after the date of admission of the will to probate or 30 days after the date of filing the probate inventory, whichever is later.

P.   Liabilities of a Personal Representative

A personal representative has the same duty of due care and loyalty to the heirs, devisees, and creditors of an estate that a trustee has to the beneficiaries of a trust. Specifically, a personal representative is liable for any loss caused to the estate arising from neglect in collecting assets of the estate or paying over money or delivering property of the estate; failure to pay taxes when due or to close the estate within a reasonable time; embezzlement or commingling of estate property; or any other wrongful act or omission.

If a personal representative breaches any of these duties, he or she can be removed, required to pay damages (known as a "surcharge"), and denied compensation.

Q.   Will Contests

A person can contest a will or claim an interest in an estate if the person believes and can prove that the will admitted to probate is ineffective, for instance, because of lack of capacity or undue influence; that there is another will; or that the decedent agreed, promised, or represented that the decedent would make or revoke a will or devise, or not revoke a will or devise, or die intestate.

A will contest or similar claim must be filed within four months after notice from the personal representative, if the person was entitled to notice. Otherwise, the contest must be filed within four months after the first publication of notice to interested persons.

Chapter 15

When You Leave a Small Estate

Oregon has several methods of settling small estates and transferring probate property without formal probate administration. The principal vehicle is the small estate affidavit. In addition, some probate property may be transferred at the owner's death without probate provided that it is the only probate property.

A. The Small Estate Affidavit

The small estate affidavit is a quick, inexpensive method of settling an estate when the property meets the qualifying limits. Generally, there must be a consensus among the heirs and devisees on how to proceed, and there must be no disputed creditor's claims or other problems that might require a court order to settle.

1. Qualifying Property

To qualify for the small estate affidavit, all the decedent's probate personal property, tangible and intangible, must have a combined fair market value of $50,000 or less, and all the probate real property must have a combined fair market value of $90,000 or less.

2. The Affidavit

The affidavit is signed by one or more "claiming successors" who are the devisees, heirs, personal representative of the decedent's will, or creditors of the estate. The affidavit must:

(a) state the name, age, domicile, post office address, and Social Security Number of the decedent;

(b) state the date and place of decedent's death;

(c) describe all the probate property and list the fair market value;

(d) state that no personal representative has been appointed;

(e) state whether or not decedent left a will;

(f) list the names and addresses of the heirs and devisees and state that a copy of the affidavit and a copy of the will, if any, will be mailed or delivered to each heir and devisee;

(g) state the interest of each heir or devisee;

(h) state that reasonable efforts have been made to ascertain all creditors of the estate, list the name, address and amount due to each claimant, including disputed claims, and state that a copy of the affidavit will be mailed to each creditor;

(i) state that a copy of the affidavit will be mailed or delivered to Adult and Family Services Division; and

(j) state that any unlisted claims or claims for more than the amounts listed will be barred if not presented within four months and that disputed claims will be barred if a petition for summary determination is not filed within four months.

A certified copy of a death certificate and the original will, if any, must be attached to the affidavit.

The affidavit cannot be filed for 30 days after the death. It is filed with the county clerk as part of the probate records in the county where the decedent died, was domiciled, or resided at the time of death, or in the county where property is located at the time of death or when the affidavit is filed. The usual filing fee is $65.

Within 30 days after the affidavit has been filed, the claiming successor must mail a copy to each heir and devisee, to each creditor whose claim has not been paid or whose claim is disputed, and to the Adult and Family Services Division, Estate Administration Section.

If the decedent owned real property, the claiming successor must sign and record a claiming successor's deed in each county where the decedent's real property is situated.

Once ten days have elapsed after the affidavit has been filed, the claiming successors may submit a copy of the affidavit to anybody who has property belonging to the decedent or who owes the decedent money. Such persons are required to deliver the property or pay over the money to the claiming successor. This includes banks holding checking or savings accounts as well as companies in which the decedent owned stock.

The claiming successor must pay claims of creditors of the decedent presented within four months after filing the affidavit. If a personal representative is not appointed for the estate within that four-month period, then at the end of the four-month period, all the property belongs outright to the persons shown in the affidavit to be entitled to it, and any other claims against the property described in the affidavit are barred. However, it is important to make certain that all heirs or devisees are included in the affidavit; if not, they could later come back and claim their share of the property, even though they were not included in the affidavit.

If there is real property, the claiming successor will eventually want to sell that property and obtain title insurance for it. One disadvantage of the small estate affidavit is that a title insurance company may charge a higher premium than it would for insuring title if the property had gone through formal probate administration. Therefore, before you use a small estate affidavit to pass title to real property, check with a title insurance company to determine what would be required to ensure marketability of the title.

B. Deposits with Financial Institutions

If the only probate property is one or more accounts at a bank, savings and loan association, or credit union, an alternative to the small estate affidavit is to submit an affidavit to the financial institution where the funds are located and obtain release of the funds without formal probate administration. Here are the rules:

(a) The amount of funds on deposit cannot exceed $25,000.

(b) The persons entitled to the funds, in order of priority, are the surviving spouse, Adult and Family Services Division (to the extent of any public assistance received by the decedent), the surviving children 18 years of age or older, the surviving parents, and surviving brothers and sisters 18 years of age or older.

(c) The affidavit must be filed by the person claiming the deposit. If the decedent died intestate without known heirs, the affidavit must be filed by the Division of State Lands.

(d) The affidavit must state where and when the decedent died and that the total deposits in all such financial institutions in Oregon do not exceed $25,000. It must show the relationship to the decedent of the party making the affidavit and must embody a promise to pay the expenses of last illness, funeral expenses, and debts out of the funds on deposit to the full extent of the funds, if necessary, and to distribute any balance to the persons entitled to it.

(e) The financial institution will transfer the funds upon receipt of the affidavit. It is under no obligation to determine the relationship of the person making the affidavit to the decedent.

(f) The transfer of funds may be made without formal probate. However, if a personal representative is appointed, the person receiving the funds is required to account for them to the personal representative.

C. Motor Vehicles

Title to motor vehicles in a deceased owner's sole name may be transferred without probate by filing with the Motor Vehicles Division an affidavit signed by all the heirs of the owner and stating the name of the person to whom ownership is to be transferred. If any heir has not reached majority or is incapacitated, a parent or guardian can sign the affidavit. The form of the affidavit is prepared by the Motor Vehicles Division. The Motor Vehicles Division will issue a new certificate and registration upon receipt of the old certificate of title, if any, the affidavit, and a registration fee.

D. Wages

Any wages up to $10,000 earned by an employee from an employer other than the State of Oregon and unpaid at the employee's death must be paid to the employee's surviving spouse, or if there is none, to the employee's dependent children, or their guardians or conservator, in equal shares.

E. Unpaid Money

Any amounts up to $10,000 due a person from the State of Oregon which are unpaid at the person's death, and any salary or wages due a deceased state employee of the State of Oregon, without limitation, may be distributed without a probate of the deceased person's estate if it is not in probate. The unpaid amount must be paid to the person's surviving spouse, or, if there is none, to the trustee of a revocable living trust created by the decedent, or, in order, to the decedent's children, parents, siblings, or nephews and nieces.

F. Real Property

If the only probate property is a parcel of real property, it is possible to transfer title to the property and give good title to a buyer without formal probate. This would normally be done only if the property were worth more than $90,000 and the small estate affidavit could not be used. This technique is conditional upon a title insurance company's willingness to insure title to the property. The following is required:

(a) There must be a sale of the property from the heirs or devisees to a third party.

(b) All heirs and devisees must be competent and willing to sign a deed or contract of sale.

(c) One or more of the heirs or devisees must submit an affidavit of heirship to the title insurance company and agree to indemnify the title insurance company against creditors' claims or claims of missing heirs.

The title insurance company will charge an additional "at risk"premium, which will usually be double the normal title insurance premium, unless the sale occurs many years after the death.

G. Savings Bonds

Under federal regulation, savings bonds of a deceased sole owner may be redeemed without probate upon submission of proper forms.

For Series EE and HH bonds, if the face amount is under $500, the bonds will be paid to the person who has paid the burial expenses and who has not been reimbursed. If the amount does not exceed $1,000, and there is no will, the bonds may be paid to the survivors in the following order of preference:

(a) spouse

(b) children or other issue

(c) parents

(d) brothers and sisters.

If the amount of the bonds is over $1,000, the proceeds may be paid to the heirs and devisees as they all agree.

H. Other Assets

There are certain assets, which do not have title documents, that may be transferred without probate administration. For instance, tangible personal property, such as furniture, stamp collections, and jewelry, do not have title documents and may be transferred without probate administration. Similarly, securities payable to bearer and not issued to the order of a specific person can be transferred by delivery.

Generally, such transfers can be accomplished without probate where there is family harmony. However, if the personal property has significant value (e.g., a valuable work of art, diamond ring, or antique), it may be necessary to go through probate to protect the property from claims of creditors or if ownership is disputed.

Chapter 16

Estate and Inheritance Taxes

When an Oregon resident dies, that person's estate may be subject to two different death taxes, the federal estate tax and the Oregon inheritance tax. In addition, if the person owns real property in a state other than Oregon, such as a condominium in Hawaii or California or a beach house in Washington, the person's estate may be subject to an estate or inheritance tax in the state where the real property is located.

The laws relating to estate and inheritances taxes are in significant transition. The 2001 federal tax act, known as the Economic Growth and Tax Relief Reconciliation Act of 2001, or EGTRRA for short, substantially increased the federal estate tax exemption and reduced the top rates beginning in 2002. These changes will occur in stages until the estate tax is repealed, for estates of persons dying in 2010.

EGTRRA also contains a sunset provision which states that the pre-2001 tax law will be reinstated in 2011. If this occurs, then the estate tax exemption, which is $1 million for 2002 and 2003, increases in stages to $3.5 million in 2009, and is repealed in 2010, will be reinstated in 2011 at $1 million. It is highly likely that sometime between now and 2011, Congress will modify the sunset provision. Here is a recap of the exemption changes:

Year	Amount Exempt
2002-03	$1 Million
2004-05	$1.5 Million
2006-08	$2 Million
2009	$3.5 Million
2010	Unlimited
2011	$1 Million

The Oregon inheritance tax law does not automatically follow federal law. For 2002 and 2003, and until the Oregon Legislative Assembly addresses the federal changes, Oregon will tax certain estates between $600,000 and $1 million, even though the federal estate tax exemption is $1 million. In its Fifth Special Session in 2002, the Oregon Legislative Assembly passed a bill which would have reconnected the Oregon inheritance tax with federal law and would have repealed it for decedent's dying after December 31, 2004. However, the Governor vetoed the measure.

Given these changes in federal law, the lingering question about the repeal of the federal estate and related tax laws, and the uncertainty about the Oregon inheritance tax law, it will be difficult for persons with taxable estates to do long-range planning with any certainty. The keys are frequent review of your estate plan and flexibility in its provisions. This chapter will explain how these laws work for estates of decedents dying in 2002 or 2003. The author will keep owners of this book updated on changes in these laws through his newsletter and website.

A. The Federal Estate Tax

Here is a summary of how to estimate and calculate the federal estate tax:

(a) calculate the gross estate;

(b) deduct all allowable deductions to get the taxable estate;

(c) add back in any taxable gifts made during the decedent's lifetime;

(d) calculate the tentative tax from the Unified Rate Schedule (see Table # 1 at the end of this chapter);

(e) deduct any gift taxes paid by the decedent to get the gross estate tax;

(f) deduct the unified credit (applicable credit amount) of $345,800, which is the equivalent of an applicable exclusion amount of $1 million (which is the estate tax exemption for 2002 and 2003); and

(g) if there is any tax due, deduct any credits, including the credit for state death taxes, to determine the net estate tax.

1. The Gross Estate

The gross estate consists of all property a person (the decedent) owned at death, plus certain property the decedent transferred during his or her life. It does not matter where the property is located, whether in one or more states or in another country, and it includes probate and nonprobate property.

Property must be reported at its fair market value. Cash, life insurance proceeds, and the like are reported at face value. Publicly traded securities are listed at the mean between their high and low on the valuation date. Other kinds of property, such as real property and works of art, generally require an appraisal.

The personal representative may elect to value real property used for farms and closely held businesses on the basis of actual use rather than fair market value. This exception is intended to relieve the burden of death taxes on farmers and other small business people who traditionally are land-rich and cash-poor.

The entire gross estate is valued either at the date of death or at the alternate valuation date. The alternate valuation date is either six months after death, or if property is sold or distributed during the six-month period, then the date of sale or distribution. You must use either the date of death for all assets or the alternate valuation date for all assets and you cannot pick and choose between the dates for different assets. The alternate valuation date is typically used in a declining market if a substantial share of the assets are not to be sold promptly after death. The alternate valuation date can be used only if its use reduces the amount of estate tax.

The value used for estate tax purposes generally fixes the basis for determining gain on a later sale for capital gains income tax purposes (see chapter 18).

2. Probate Property

Probate property owned in the decedent's name alone is listed on the federal estate return at full value. Property owned by the decedent as tenants in common with another person is listed with the fair market value of the decedent's portion.

The following kinds of probate property should be included:

(a) real property, including property being bought on contract;

(b) all stocks and bonds including savings bonds or other government securities;

(c) interests in a family-owned business, such as stock in a corporation, a partnership interest, or a membership interest in a limited liability company;

(d) all notes, mortgages, and trust deeds being paid to the decedent;

(e) all cash on hand;

(f) household goods, jewelry, royalty rights, remainders and judgments; and

(g) any other probate property.

3. Joint and Survivorship Property

Property owned jointly with right of survivorship by the decedent and another person must be reported on the estate tax return at its full value. If the property was owned jointly by the decedent and a surviving spouse who is a U.S. citizen, then one-half is included and one-half excluded, regardless of which spouse provided the consideration for the purchase.

A different rule applies for property owned jointly with right of survivorship by persons who are not married to each other or by a decedent and a surviving spouse who is not a U.S. citizen (even if the surviving spouse is a permanent resident of the United States). The full value of the jointly owned property must be included unless: (1) the surviving joint owner can prove that he or she originally owned all or part of the property or furnished part of the consideration for its acquisition; or (2) the two owners received the property jointly as an inheritance, devise, or gift from someone else.

4. Property Transferred Before Death

Federal estate tax is imposed on certain transfers of property that the decedent made while still alive. At one time all gifts made during the three-year period prior to death were considered owned by the decedent at death and included in the gross estate. However, now only certain transfers made prior to death are included in the gross estate. The principal ones are:

(a) any federal gift taxes paid on gifts made during the three years before death;

(b) the full amount of the proceeds of any life insurance policy given away during the three years before the death;

(c) the value of any property over which the decedent had a power of appointment if the decedent relinquished that power during the three years before death;

(d) the value of any property transferred during the decedent's lifetime in which the decedent reserved a life estate and

(e) lifetime transfers in which the decedent reserved the right to amend or revoke, such as assets in a revocable living trust.

5. Other Nonprobate Property

The following nonprobate property is included in the gross estate:

(a) the full amount of the proceeds of all life insurance policies on the decedent's life which the decedent owned, or over which the decedent had "incidents of ownership"(such as the right to change beneficiaries) at date of death;

(b) annuities, IRAs, and other retirement benefits;

(c) POD (payable on death), TOD (transfer on death) and ITF (in trust for) accounts and securities; and

(d) the value of any property over which the decedent had a general power of appointment.

B. Deductions

Deductions that can be made from the gross estate are:

(a) funeral expenses;

(b) personal representative's fees;

(c) attorney fees and other administration expenses;

(d) all unpaid income and property taxes, notes secured by a mortgage, and other debts;

(e) net losses during administration, such as losses from theft, fire, or storm not reimbursed by insurance;

(f) property passing to a surviving spouse who is a U.S. citizen. There is an unlimited marital deduction if the gift is not just an interest for life only. Property placed in certain special trusts for a surviving spouse, such as a Q-TIP (qualified terminable interest property) trust, also qualifies for the marital deduction.

(g) property for a surviving spouse who is not a U.S. citizen (even if the spouse is a U.S. resident), provided it is in a special trust, known as a "qualified domestic trust."or "QDOT"for short. Outright transfers to a noncitizen spouse, such as under a will, or nonprobate transfers, such as life insurance proceeds not in trust, do not qualify for the marital deduction unless the non-citizen spouse becomes a citizen or agrees to place the property in a QDOT.

(h) gifts or irrevocable lifetime trusts to qualified charities.

C. Calculating the Tax

After deductions have been subtracted from the gross estate, add any lifetime taxable gifts made by the decedent. A taxable gift is any present gift in excess of the annual exclusion and any gift which does not qualify as a "present interest" such as a gift to an irrevocable trust or a gift of a remainder interest. The gift tax annual exclusion was $3,000 per year before 1982, $10,000 per year from 1981 through 2001 and is $11,000 per year beginning in 2002. With the new total, calculate the "tentative tax" from Table # 1.

Next, deduct from the tentative tax due any gift taxes that the decedent paid for lifetime gifts and the unified credit of $345,800 (which is the equivalent estate tax exemption of $1 million). The federal gift and estate tax exemptions and rates are unified in the sense that if a person makes lifetime taxable gifts (basically any gift worth more than $11,000 to one person in one year), any excess applies against the combined lifetime and death tax exemption of $1million. This is why taxable gifts are added to the taxable estate and gift taxes paid are deducted from the tentative tax.

For instance, if a person made a lifetime gift of $71,000 to one donee, the person would have used $60,000 of the $1 million exemption (after deduction of the annual exclusion of $11,000), leaving $940,000 of the exemption for later lifetime gifts or as a credit against the estate tax. A person pays no gift tax until taxable gifts exceed the exemption of $1 million, after which there would be no credit left against the estate tax.

If there is a tax due after deduction of the exemption, you may deduct a state death tax credit. For estates of persons dying in 2002, the credit is either the amount of the state death tax payable to Oregon or 75% of the maximum credit calculated in accordance with Table #2, whichever is less. For estates of persons dying in 2003, the deduction cannot exceed 50% of the maximum credit.

Because Oregon imposes a tax equal to 100 percent of the maximum credit, the estate of an Oregon decedent will always be able to deduct the maximum credit.

There are several other credits against the estate tax, such as a credit for foreign death taxes and a credit for prior transfers, but they are rarely available.

If after deduction of all credits there is a tax due, the marginal rate will range from 41% to 50%.

D.   Filing the Return and Paying the Tax

An estate tax return (form 706) must be filed for every estate in which the gross estate equals or exceeds the estate tax exemption, which is $1 million for 2002 and 2003. A return must be filed if the gross estate meets this threshold amount, even if the taxable estate is less than $1 million and no tax is due. The return must be filed within nine months after death, but a reasonable extension may be obtained for good cause.

Any federal estate tax due must also be paid within nine months after death unless an extension of time to pay is obtained. An extension of time to file the return does not automatically extend the time to pay the tax. The IRS has discretion to extend the time to pay for up to ten years after the due date for reasonable cause, such as lack of cash and inability to sell estate property except at a substantial loss to the estate. An estate, as a matter of right, may defer a portion of the estate tax for up to 14 years at 4% interest if the tax is on certain qualifying closely held businesses.

E.   The Oregon Inheritance Tax

Oregon imposes an inheritance tax, called a "pick-up" tax, equal to the maximum federal state death tax credit. If the decedent leaves property subject to death tax in Oregon and one or more other states, the credit will be apportioned among the states, and Oregon will require payment of its proportionate share of the tax. The tax is due nine months after death, which is the same due date as the due date for the federal estate tax return.

Changes in federal estate tax law are not automatically incorporated into Oregon law and become part of Oregon law only if approved by the Oregon Legislative Assembly. The federal law changes enacted by EGTRRA will not become part of Oregon law until the Oregon Legislative Assembly addresses these changes, probably in its 2003 session. In addition, the Oregon Department of Revenue has determined that the federal estate tax changes made by the Taxpayer Relief Act of 97 (TRA 97) have not been approved by the Oregon Legislative Assembly.

For estates of decedents dying in 2002 and possibly also for decedents dying in 2003, Oregon will impose an inheritance tax based on federal law as it existed before EGTRRA and before TRA 97. Under prior federal tax law, the estate tax exemption for 2002 and 2003 would have been $600,000. Oregon will therefore impose an inheritance tax on some estates valued between $600,000 and $1 million even though there will be no federal estate tax to pay.

Oregon will impose an inheritance tax only if an estate is required to file a federal estate tax return. Under federal law, a federal estate tax return must be filed if the gross estate is $1 million or more. The filing requirement is based on the value of the federal gross estate, not the taxable estate. In effect, an estate must file a return if a decedent's assets are worth $1 million or more, even though a decedent's net worth (assets less liabilities) is less than that amount.

In summary, Oregon will impose an inheritance tax even though no federal estate tax is due if: (1) a decedent's gross estate is $1 million or more; and (2) the taxable estate is between $600,000 and $1 million. However, Oregon will not impose an inheritance tax if a decedent's gross estate is less than $1 million, even though the taxable estate is between $600,000 and $1 million.

There will be disparities in the imposition of the Oregon inheritance tax for decedents dying in 2002. For example, suppose the gross estate were $1,100,000, but the taxable estate were $900,000. A federal estate tax return would have to be filed, but no estate tax due. However, because a federal estate tax return must be filed, the estate would have to pay an Oregon inheritance tax of $30,400. If the gross estate were $950,000 instead of $1,100,000 and the taxable estate were the same $900,000, no federal estate tax return would have be filed and therefore no Oregon inheritance tax due.

EGTRRA will phase out the state death tax credit over three years, allowing 75% of the credit against the gross estate tax for estates of decedents dying in 2002, 50% for 2003, and 25% for 2004. From 2005 through 2009 the credit will be replaced by an unlimited estate tax deduction. For 2002 and 2003, however, Oregon will base its pick-up tax on 100% of the maximum state death tax credit

Table #3 lists the combined estimated federal and Oregon death taxes at various levels of taxable estates for estates of decedents dying in 2002.

F.   Generation Skipping Transfer Tax

In addition to the federal estate tax, federal law also imposes a tax on transfers that skip a generation (for instance, a gift from a grandparent to a grandchild). The tax is a flat rate equal to the maximum estate and gift tax rate (currently 50%). There is a $1 million per transferor exemption which is indexed for inflation. For 2002, the exemption is $1,100,000. Beginning in 2004 the exemption will increase at the same rate as the estate tax exemption. The tax will be repealed in its entirety in 2010, and the exemption will be reinstated in 2011 at $1,100,000.

G.   Married Couples and Bypass Trusts

For a married couple with combined taxable estates over $1 million, use of a bypass trust, sometimes called a credit-shelter trust, at the death of the spouse first to die can minimize or eliminate death taxes in both estates.

For example, suppose a married couple with a net worth of $2 million have typical mom-and-pop wills leaving all their property to each other, then to their children after both have died. There would be no death taxes on the first death because of the unlimited marital deduction. However, death taxes on the surviving spouse's death on an estate of $2 million at 2002 rates would be about $460,000.

Suppose instead that the couple provided, either in their wills or living trusts, that on the first death $1 million worth of assets would go into a trust for the surviving spouse. The trust would be for the surviving spouse's benefit during his or her lifetime, then go to the children after the surviving spouse's death. There would be no tax on the first spouse's death because the assets going into the trust are exempt under the first spouse's $1 million exemption.

Upon the surviving spouse's death, the assets in the trust would not be taxed in the surviving spouse's estate because the surviving spouse would not have complete control over the assets.

Those assets "bypass"the surviving spouse's estate for estate tax purposes. The other $1 million of assets owned by the surviving spouse would be exempt under the surviving spouse's exemption. By making use of both $1 million exemptions, the couple would save their children $ 460,000 in death taxes (at 2002 rates).

Table #1
Unified Rate Schedule
(2002 & 2003)

Column A	Column B	Column C	Column D
Taxable Amount Over	Taxable Amount Not Over	Tax On Amount In Column A	Rate of tax on excess over amount in Column A
			(Percent)
500,000	750,000	155,800	37
750,000	1,000,000	248,300	39
1,000,000	1,250,000	345,800	41
1,250,000	1,500,000	448,300	43
1,500,000	2,000,000	555,800	45
2,000,000	2,500,000	780,000	49
2,500,000	3,000,000	1,025,800	50

Note: In 2003 the top rate will decline to 49% for taxable estates of $2 million or more.

Table #2
Maximum Credit for State Death Taxes
(Based on federal adjusted taxable estate which is the
federal taxable estate reduced by $60,000)
(2002 & 2003)

Column 1	Column 2	Column 3	Column 4
Adjusted taxable estate equal to or more than —	Adjusted taxable estate less than —	Credit on amount in Column (1)	Rate of credit on estate over amount in Column (1)
640,000	840,000	18,000	4.8
840,000	1,040,000	27,600	5.6
1,040,000	1,540,000	38,800	6.4
1,540,000	2,040,000	70,800	7.2
2,040,000	2,540,000	106,800	8.0
2,540,000	3,040,000	146,800	8.8
3,040,000	3,540,000	190,800	9.6
3,540,000	4,040,000	238,800	10.4
4,040,000	5,040,000	290,800	11.2
5,040,000	6,040,000	402,800	12.0
6,040,000	7,040,000	522,800	12.8
7,040,000	8,040,000	650,800	13.6
8,040,000	9,040,000	786,800	14.4
9,040,000	10,040,000	930,800	15.2
10,040,000	–	1,082,800	16.0

Table #3
Combined Federal Estate and Oregon Inheritance Taxes
(2002)

Taxable Estate	Tentative Federal Estate Tax	75% of S.D.T.C.	Net Federal Estate Tax	Oregon Inheritance Tax (S.D.T.C.)	Total Taxes
650,000	-0-	-0-	-0-	16,000	16,000
700,000	-0-	-0-	-0-	18,000	18,000
750,000	-0-	-0-	-0-	18,500	18,500
800,000	-0-	-0-	-0-	22,800	22,800
900,000	-0-	-0-	-0-	27,600	27,600
1,000,000	-0-	-0-	-0-	33,200	33,200
1,250,000	102,500	36,300	66,200	48,400	114,600
1,500,000	210,000	48,300	161,700	64,400	226,100
2,000,000	435,000	74,700	360,300	99,600	459,900
2,500,000	680,000	104,100	575,900	138,800	714,700
3,000,000	930,000	136,500	793,500	182,000	975,500
3,500,000	1,180,000	171,200	1,008,800	229,200	1,238,000
4,000,000	1,430,000	210,300	1,219,700	280,400	1,500,100
5,000,000	1,930,000	293,700	1,636,300	391,600	2,027,900
6,000,000	2,430,000	383,100	2,046,900	510,800	2,557,700
7,000,000	2,930,000	478,500	2,451,500	638,000	3,089,500
8,000,000	3,430,000	579,900	2,850,100	773,200	3,623,300

S.D.T.C. = State Death Tax Credit

Chapter 17

Gift Taxes During Your Lifetime

A. The Federal Gift Tax

Federal law imposes a tax on the lifetime transfer of any property that has monetary value from one person (the donor) to another person (the donee) for no consideration, or for consideration that is less than the value of the property given. There are four elements to a taxable gift:

(a) The donor and donee must be competent.

(b) The donor must intend to give up title and control of the property.

(c) There must be a voluntary irrevocable transfer or delivery of the property.

(d) The gifted property must be accepted by the donee.

1. Kinds of Gifts

An outright gift might be cash, securities, or a house where title is transferred from the donor's name to the donee's sole name.

The creation of a joint interest, such as a tenancy in common, can be a gift. If the donor conveys title to a house from the donor's sole name to the donee so they each own an undivided half interest as tenants in common, the donor has made a gift of one-half of the value of the property. If a donor conveys a remainder interest to the donee, reserving a life estate, the donor has made a gift of the value of the property less the actuarial value of the life estate.

A sale of property for less than fair market value is a bargain sale and is considered a gift. If you sell a house that is worth $75,000 to your daughter for $50,000, you have made a gift to her of $25,000. This rule does not apply when it is an arm's length sale to a non-relative.

If you set up an irrevocable lifetime trust and transfer property to the trustee, you have made a gift for tax purposes. This does not apply to transfers to a revocable trust since you do not give up control of the property.

If you pay off a debt owed by another person, such as paying off a grandchild's car loan, you make an indirect gift to the grandchild.

2. Excluded Gifts

All gifts are subject to gift tax unless they are specifically excluded. There are three categories of excluded gifts: marital and charitable gifts, tuition and medical expense payments, and annual exclusion gifts.

Marital and charitable gifts. There is an unlimited exclusion for gifts to qualified charities and gifts to a citizen spouse. However, a gift to a citizen spouse that is limited or terminable, such as a life estate, does not qualify for the marital deduction. Gifts to a noncitizen spouse are excluded from the gift tax only up to $100,000 annually, adjusted for inflation. For 2002, the exclusion is $110,000.

Tuition and medical expense payments. There is an unlimited exclusion for tuition and medical payments for another person. Tuition payments must be made directly to the educational institution and not to the student. Medical payments must be made directly to the provider of the medical services.

Annual exclusion gifts. For annual exclusion gifts, you are allowed one annual exclusion per year per donee. If you make more than one gift in a single year to one donee, the gifts must be totaled together to determine whether you are within the exclusion. The amount of annual exclusion is adjusted periodically for inflation. For 2002, the annual exclusion is $11,000.

There is no limit to the number of donees you may have. If you wanted to give $11,000 to each of five different persons in one year, for a total of $55,000, you would not have made a taxable gift because of the annual exclusion.

A husband and wife may split their gifts and use both their annual exclusions and their unified credits. For example, if a husband wants to make a gift of $22,000 of his own property, and his wife consents to the gift, the gift will be treated as having been given half by each spouse. If a husband and wife elect gift splitting, they become jointly liable for the gift tax for that calendar year.

To qualify for the annual exclusion, the gift must be of a present interest and not a future interest. For example, a gift of a remainder interest in a house is a future interest and does not qualify for the annual exclusion.

3. Calculating the Gift Tax

If you make a gift in excess of the annual exclusion, then the balance applies toward your lifetime gift tax exemption of $1 million. For instance, suppose you gave your son a house worth $111,000 and that you had never made any taxable gifts before this gift. A portion of the gift equal to $11, 000 would qualify for the annual exclusion. The balance of $100,000 would reduce your lifetime exemption from $1 million to $900,000. You would pay no gift tax. If you made no additional taxable gifts during your lifetime, then at your death you would have an estate tax exemption of $900,000. You do not pay gift tax unless the cumulative total of taxable gifts you have made during your lifetime exceeds your lifetime exemption, also called the applicable exclusion amount, $1 million.

4. Reporting Gifts

You must file a gift tax return any year in which you make one or more gifts of a present interest which in total exceed the annual exclusion in value ($11,000 for 2002) to any one donee, or any year in which you make a gift of a future interest. You must file the gift tax return and pay any gift tax due by April 15 following the year of the gift.

Gifts must be reported for gift tax purposes at fair market value at the date of the gift. Gifts of a partial interest in property are reported at the value of the partial interest. For instance, suppose a 50-year-old male made a gift of a remainder interest in a house worth $100,000, reserving a life estate, and the current federal rate was 8%. Based on actuarial tables, the value of the remainder interest, which would be reported for gift tax purposes, would be $17,697.

5. Lifetime Gifts and Basis

The rules requiring an adjustment in basis when a person dies (see chapter 18) do not apply to lifetime gifts.

For example, if you gave your son a house you purchased for $11,000, and he sold it for $111,000, he would have a capital gain to report of $100,000. This rule applies, even if your son were to sell the house after you died. If instead, your son inherited the house from you after you died, the house were worth $111,000 at your death, and he sold it for $111,000, he would have no capital gains to report.

As a general rule, if you are going to make lifetime gifts, you should first consider cash or assets with high basis before giving away assets with low basis.

6. Changes in Federal Gift Tax Law

EGTRRA, the federal tax act passed in 2001, which repealed the estate tax effective in 2010, did not repeal the federal gift tax. Beginning in 2002, the total amount of taxable gifts which can be made without gift tax liability is $1 million. This gift tax lifetime exemption will not increase with the estate tax exemption and will not be repealed in 2010. Any taxable gifts in excess of this $1 million exemption will be taxed at a flat rate of 35%.

B. The Oregon Gift Tax

Oregon has repealed its gift tax and does not impose a tax on lifetime voluntary transfers made after December 31, 1986.

Chapter 18

Death and Income Taxes

When property which constitutes a capital asset is inherited from a decedent, the basis of property for income tax purposes is adjusted to its fair market value at the date of decedent's death. If the value of the property at date of death is higher than the decedent's basis, then the basis is stepped up to that value; if it is lower, it is stepped down to the lower value. This value is used as the basis for later sale, and, for depreciable property, the basis after death for calculating depreciation.

For instance, suppose Ted dies owning 100 shares of ABC Corporation stock, which he purchased for $300 several years prior to his death. At his death the stock is worth $1,500. In his will Ted gives the stock to his daughter, Alice, who later sells it for $2,000. If Ted had sold the stock during his lifetime for $2,000, he would have had to report a gain of $1,700 for capital gains purposes, the difference between his cost of $300 and the sales price of $2,000. Alice, however, will have to report a gain of only $500, the difference between the date-of-death value of $1,500 and the sales price of $2,000. The appreciation in value during Ted's lifetime from his cost of $300 to $1,500 is thus sheltered from capital gains tax.

A. Property Subject to Basis Change

Property subject to the change in basis rule must be acquired from the decedent by reason of the decedent's death and must be includible in the decedent's gross estate for federal estate tax purposes, regardless of whether or not a federal estate tax return is filed. The primary types of property are probate property, property owned jointly by the decedent and another person with right of survivorship and other property includible in the decedent's estate, such as property in the decedent's revocable living trust and property in which decedent reserved a life estate.

If a federal estate tax return is filed, then generally the values listed in the estate tax return for estate tax purposes are also used for determining the basis at date of death for income tax purposes. If the alternate valuation date is elected (see chapter 16), then the fair market values for basis purposes are the values on the alternate valuation date. If no estate tax return is filed, then fair market values for basis purposes are based on appraisal or other means.

It is important to determine valuations whenever a person dies and keep a record of those valuations for later sale, even if no estate tax return is filed. If you inherit property and guess or estimate its date-of-death value when you sell the property later, and that guess is substantially higher than its actual value, you may be subject to overvaluation penalties.

B. Joint and Survivorship Property

Special rules apply for property owned jointly with right of survivorship by the decedent and another person.

For property owned jointly with right of survivorship by a decedent and a citizen spouse, the rule for estate tax purposes is that half of the value is included and half excluded. This "fifty-fifty" rule means that for basis purposes the decedent's half of joint and survivorship property is its fair market value at death and the other half is the surviving spouse's cost or other basis in the property.

For example, suppose that George and Martha own 100 shares of ABC Corporation, which they purchased for $300. Martha dies first, and at her death, the stock is worth $1,500. One-half of this amount, or $750, is includible in Martha's estate for estate tax purposes. George later sells the stock for $2,000.

To determine his gain, George has to split the basis. One half of the basis, the half that was includible in Martha's estate at her death, is $750. The other half is one-half of the original cost of $300, or $150, representing George's half. The total basis is $900 ($750 plus $150), so George has to report a gain of $1,100, the difference between the sales price of $2,000 and his basis of $900.

A different rule, known as the "consideration furnished"rule, applies to property owned jointly with right of survivorship by a decedent and a noncitizen spouse or by a decedent and another joint owner who is not the decedent's spouse. For estate tax purposes, the full value of the property is includible in the estate of the joint owner first to die unless the surviving joint owner can show that he or she furnished all or part of the consideration for the purchase of the property.

Suppose, in our example above, that George and Martha were brother and sister and that Martha had purchased the stock with her own funds and had then added George's name as a joint owner. At Martha's death, the full value of the stock, $1,500, would have been includible in her estate. This means that when George later sold the stock for $2,000, his basis would have been $1,500 and his gain $500. If George had died first and Martha later sells the stock for $2,000, her basis would be the original cost basis of $300 and her gain $1,700.

The "fifty-fifty" rule, which applies to most married couples, works to their disadvantage when the spouse first to die provides all the consideration for the purchase of the property, because the rule applies regardless of who furnished the consideration. For estate tax purposes, the fifty-fifty rule has little effect because the fifty percent share that is includible in the deceased spouse's estate qualifies for the estate tax marital deduction. If the "consideration furnished"rule applied and 100% of the value of property were includible in the deceased spouse's estate, there would still be no estate tax to pay because of the unlimited marital deduction, and the surviving spouse would receive a 100% instead of a 50% step-up in basis for income tax purpose for property which had appreciated in value.

Prior to 1977, the "consideration furnished" rule applied to married couples where the surviving spouse was a citizen. A series of court rulings have held that if such a married couple purchased property prior to 1977, the "consideration furnished" rule applies, even though the property is sold after 1977. This means that if the spouse first to die is the spouse who furnished the consideration for the purchase of the property, then when the surviving spouse later sells the property, he or she can claim a 100% step-up in the basis of the property.

C.   Carryover Basis After 2009

EGTRRA, the 2001 tax act, repealed the step-up in basis rules for appreciated capital gains property for decedents dying after 2009. After that date an estate can allocate $1.3 million in "aggregate basis increase"among the decedent's assets. This does not mean that property worth $1.3 million may be stepped up to fair market value; rather that the allocated property may have its basis increased up to an aggregate increase of $1.3 million. Property passing to a surviving citizen spouse is subject to an additional basis increase of $3 million. Any property of the decedent which does not receive a step-up in basis under these rules will carry over the decedent's basis. It is important for persons with substantial estates who may be subject to these new rules to keep accurate records of the cost or other basis information of their property.

D.   Property Not Subject to Basis Change

Income to which a decedent is entitled but which a decedent does not receive prior to death does not receive a basis adjustment at death. Such income must be reported when received either by the estate or by the beneficiaries, and it has the same character in the hands of the recipient as it did in the hands of the decedent. This income is known as "income with respect to a decedent" or "IRD" for short.

Common examples of IRD are:

(a) IRAs (other than nondeductible contributions) and other retirement benefits;

(b) unpaid salaries, bonuses, deferred compensation and stock options;

(c) installment sales receivable and gains on property sales which are pending at death and not closed until after death;

(d) accrued, but unpaid, dividends and interest, including interest on savings bonds; and

(e) crops, livestock, business inventory and accounts receivable.

IRD property is includible in a decedent's estate for estate tax purposes, and is thus subject both to income and to estate taxation at death. To mitigate this double tax burden, federal tax law permits a deduction for income tax purposes for estate tax attributable to the IRD property.

Naming a qualified charity as a beneficiary of IRD property is an especially effective planning tool because it can save both income and estate taxation.

Glossary

Ademption – The rule which states that if property which is specifically given or devised to a person in a will is destroyed, sold or given away by the testator after the date of the will and before the testator's death, the devise fails and the person does not receive the property or its equivalent value. In such case the property *adeems*. Also called a*demption by extinction.* Certain exceptions to this rele are known as *nonademption of specific devises.*

Administration – A court-supervised proceeding for transferring your property on your death. (See also PROBATE ADMINIS-TRATION.)

Advance Directive – Form which a person can sign naming health care representatives and directing how health care decisions are to be made for a person in case of a person's incapacity.

Agency Account – A special form of deposit account with a financial institution, similar to a power of attorney.

Ancillary Probate – A second probate administration in another state. This commonly occurs when the decedent owns probate real property in more than one state.

Annuity – A contract providing for yearly (or monthly) payments.

Antenuptial Agreement – See PREMARITAL AGREEMENT

Antilapse – Refers to the rule that determines who gets property given to a devisee under a will who predeceases the testator.

Attestation Clause – The clause signed by witnesses to a will.

Attorney-in-Fact – An agent authorized to act under a power of attorney; to be distinguished from an attorney at law, who is a person authorized to represent a party in a legal matter (a lawyer).

Beneficiary – (a) A person for whom a trust is established (see also TRUST.)

(b) The recipient of life insurance proceeds.

(c) The recipient of property under a will.

Bequeath – To dispose of personal property in a will. This term is now archaic and is usually referred to as devise.

Bequest – A disposition of personal property by will; usually called a devise.

Certification of Trust – A form, to be signed by a trustee of a trust, providing a summary of information about the trust and the trustee's authority.

Codicil – An amendment to a will.

Community Property – A form of property ownership between married persons under the laws of certain states other than Oregon. Oregon is known as a *common-law* state.

Conservatorship – A court-supervised legal proceeding to handle and protect the property and affairs of a minor or incapacitated person. The person appointed to handle the affairs is called a *conservator* (formerly called a *guardian of the estate*). The person for whom the conservatorship is set up is called the *protected* person.

Corporation – An artificial legal entity created by state law and used for conducting business.

Custodianship – A procedure, not supervised by the court, for managing property of minors. A *custodian* is the person handling the property.

Decedent – A person who has died leaving property subject to probate administration; more generally a deceased person.

Declaration for Mental Health Treatment – A form which a person can sign directing how certain mental health decisions would be made for a person if a person becomes incapacitated.

Deed – A document by which you transfer or convey title to real property. The person conveying the property is called the *grantor*. The recipient of the property is called the *grantee*. For a conveyance of real property to be legally effective, the deed must be both signed by the grantor and delivered to the grantee. The deed should also be recorded. There are four types of deeds in Oregon, a quit claim deed, a bargain and sale deed, a warranty deed, and a special warranty deed.

Descent and Distribution – Another name for intestate succession.

Devise – To dispose of property by will (verb). A disposition of property by will (noun). There are three types of devises:

   (a) Specific devise – A devise of a specific thing (e.g., rings or jewelry)

   (b) General devise – A devise that is chargeable generally on your estate or property (e.g., a gift of $1,000).

   (c) Residue – All probate property of an estate except property that constitutes a general or specific devise.

Devisee – A recipient of property under the will.

Directive to Physicians – A document by which you direct your physician not to use artificial means to keep you alive if you are terminally ill; now obsolete; see Advance Directive.

Disclaimer – A renunciation of a right to receive property whether under a will, trust, or other document.

Disinherit – To omit from your will a person who would have been an heir and would have received a share of your estate under the rules of intestate succession had you died without a will.

Distributee – A person entitled to property of a decedent either as a devisee under a will or, if there is no will, as an heir under intestate succession.

Escheat – The rule of intestate succession that if a person dies without a will and with no heirs, all his or her probate property goes to the state.

Estate – All of a person's property or interest in property, real or personal. A person's probate estate is the person's probate property. The *taxable* estate is all property subject to estate or inheritance tax.

Estate Planning – Planning the disposition of your property at death including preparation of a will, taking steps to minimize death taxes, and making certain all affairs and documents, such as title to property and designation of beneficiaries of life insurance policies, are in order.

Executor/Executrix – The names for a male or female personal representative named in the will.

Exordium Clause – The opening clause of a will.

Fee Title or **Fee Simple** – A form of ownership of real property in which only one person has any interest. This may be contrasted with a life estate, remainder interest, or tenancy by the entirety.

Fiduciary – A person who holds property in trust for another or who has a special relationship of trust to another. A personal representative, conservator, guardian, trustee, custodian and attorney in fact each stand in such a relationship.

Grantee – A person who receives a conveyance of real property.

Grantor – (a) A person who conveys title to real property by means of a deed.

(b) A person who sets up a trust; trustor.

Guardian – A person appointed by a court and charged with the care and well-being of a minor or an incapacitated adult. The person for whom a guardian is appointed is called the *protected person*.

Heir – Any person, including a surviving spouse, entitled under the laws of intestate success/on to the probate property of a decedent who died wholly or partially intestate.

Holographic Will – A handwritten, unwitnessed will; not valid in Oregon.

Intangible Personal Property – Stocks and bonds, bank accounts, life insurance, etc.

Inter Vivos Trust – A trust created and funded by a trustor while the trustor is still alive; also called a living trust.

Intestate – Without a will. A person dies intestate if he or she dies without a valid will.

Intestate Succession – The law that determines who will get your property on your death and who will be appointed the personal representative of your estate if you die with probate property and without a will.

Irrevocable Trust – A living trust in which the trustee gives up control of the property and cannot get it back.

Issue – See LINEAL DESCENDANTS

Joint Account – A multiparty deposit account with a financial institution.

Joint Tenancy/Joint Tenancy with Right of Survivorship – Two closely-related forms of joint ownership of personal property with right of survivorship.

Joint Will/Joint and Mutual Wills – Wills of a married couple contained in a single document; now rare.

Letters of Administration – A court document certifying a person's appointment as an administrator or administratrix.

Letters Testamentary – A court document certifying a person's appointment as an executor or executrix.

Life Estate and Remainder – A form of property ownership in which two or more persons have an interest in the property. The first person, the *life tenant,* is entitled to sole possession for life. Upon his or her death, the other person, the *remainderman,* has sole title and right to possession of the property.

Limited Liability Company – A form of business entity which combines the limited liability protection of a corporation with the income tax treatment of a partnership.

Lineal Descendants – Lineal descendants are a person's children, grandchildren, great-grandchildren, and any others who are in the same line of descent or subsequent generations. *Issue* has a more limited definition. It includes all lineal descendants except those who are lineal descendants of living descendants.

Living Trust – A trust created and funded by a trustor while the trustor is still alive; also called an *inter vivos* trust.

Living Will – See DIRECTIVE TO PHYSICIANS.

Minor – In Oregon, generally an unmarried person under age 18.

Mortgage – A document given by the owner of real property to a lender or seller to secure payment of an obligation and to create a lien against the property. Similar to a trust deed.

Nonprobate Property – Property not subject to probate administration.

Nuncupative Will – An oral will later reduced to writing but not signed by the testator; not valid in Oregon.

Partnership – An association of two or more persons to carry on a business for profit as co-owners. A partnership agreement may be written or oral.

Personal Property – All property that is not real property.

Personal Representative – A person or trust company appointed by a probate court to administer a decedent's estate.

    (a) Executor/executrix: The title given a personal representative who is named in the decedent's will.

    (b) Administrator/administratrix: The title given a personal representative if the decedent died without a will.

    (c) Administrator/administratrix with will annexed: The title given a personal representative when the decedent dies with a will in which decedent fails to designate a personal representative or the personal representative is dead or otherwise fails to act.

    (d) Administrator de bonis non: A successor personal representative.

Postnuptial Agreement – An agreement between a married couple concerning their property and entered into after their marriage. It can also be called a marital property agreement.

Pour-Over Will – A will signed in conjunction with a living trust. The will provides that upon your death any probate property will be transferred to or "poured over" to the living trust.

Power of Appointment – A power granted in a trust to a person, called the *donee* or *holder* of the power, to direct who receives trust property.

Power of Attorney – A document authorizing someone to act as your agent. That person is called your *attorney-in-fact*. You are the *principal*. A power of attorney may be general or limited. A power of attorney is *durable* if it is effective during the principal's incapacity. Generally a person will have one power of attorney for health care and a separate power of attorney for property and financial management.

Precatory – Language in a will that is a suggestion to your personal representative but is not legally binding on him or her.

Premarital Agreement – An agreement between a couple concerning their property and entered into before their marriage. Also called a *prenuptial agreement* or *antenuptial agreement*.

Pretermitted Child – A child inadvertently left out of your will.

Probate Administration – A court-supervised proceeding to transfer your probate property on your death from your name to the persons who are legally entitled to it, either under your will or pursuant to law.

Property – Anything of value or capable of being owned. All property may be categorized as follows:

(a) Real property: Land and buildings or other fixtures permanently affixed to the land.

(b) Personal property: All property that is not real property.

(c) Tangible personal property: Furniture, clothing, motor vehicles, and the like.

(d) Intangible personal property: Stocks and bonds, bank accounts, life insurance, contract fights, and the like.

(e) Probate property: Property subject to probate administration.

(f) Nonprobate property: Property not subject to probate administration.

Real Property – Land and buildings on the land.

Remainder – (a) See LIFE ESTATE.
(b) Another word for residue.

Representation – A rule determining which heirs inherit from a person dying intestate when the heirs are of unequal kinship.

Residue – See DEVISE

Revocable Trust – A form of living trust that the trustor may revoke during his or her lifetime.

Sibling – A brother or sister.

Specific Devise – See DEVISE

Spendthrift – A person who cannot manage his or her financial affairs and spends money extravagantly or wastefully.

Spouse – A husband or wife.

Tenancy by the Entirety – Form of joint real property ownership by married persons.

Tenancy in Common – A form of joint ownership involving two or more persons each owning an undivided interest, but with no right of survivorship. Each joint owner is called a *tenant in common.*

Testamentary Capacity – The mental capacity required to make, amend, or revoke a will.

Testamentary Trust – A trust set up in a will or in the post-death part of a living trust and coming into effect after the death of the testator or trustor.

Testimonium Clause – The clause in your will that states that you have signed it.

Testate – With a will. A person dies testate if he or she dies with a valid will. Otherwise he or she dies intestate.

Testator – A man who makes a will.

Testatrix – A woman who makes a will.

Totten Trust – A form of bank account that you set up in your name as trustee for someone else, called the beneficiary, and is revocable while you are living.

Trust – A trust is an arrangement in which one person known as the *grantor, settlor,* or *trustor* transfers property to another person or entity, known as the *trustee,* who administers the property for the benefit of some other person, known as the *beneficiary.* The trustor may be the beneficiary.

(a) Living (inter vivos) trust: A trust in which the trustor transfers property to the trustee while the trustor is still alive.

(b) Testamentary trust: A trust set up in a person's will or in the post-death portion of a person's living trust.

(c) Revocable trust: A form of living trust under which the trustor may terminate or revoke the trust during his or her lifetime.

(d) Standby trust: A form of revocable living trust.

(e) Irrevocable trust: A form of living trust under which the trustor cannot terminate or revoke. The trustor gives up all or most control of the property and cannot get it back.

(f) Sprinkling or spray trust: A trust under which the trustee is permitted to make unequal distributions to the beneficiaries.

Trust Account – A form of multi-party deposit account with a financial institution.

Trust Company – A bank or other financial institution authorized by state law to engage in trust business.

Trust Deed – A document given by the owner of real property to a trustee in trust to secure payment of an obligation given by the grantor to a beneficiary, and creating a lien against the property; similar to a mortgage.

Trustee – Someone who administers property for another's benefit.

Trustor – A person who transfers property in trust to another person.

Undue Influence – Improper influence on a person making a will that invalidates the will.

Will – A written declaration of a person's intentions concerning the disposition of his or her probate property at death.

Contacting the Author

Newsletter

The author publishes a newsletter once or twice a year which he mails to his clients and to owners of this book to keep them current on changes in the law concerning wills, trusts and estate planning as they relate to Oregon residents. The newsletter also serves as an update of this book. There is no charge for the newsletter. If you have purchased this book and would like to receive the newsletter, contact the author.

Website

The author maintains a website, which contains articles from his newsletter and other articles relating to estate planning. The website address is www.rcjlaw.com.

Seminars

The author gives free monthly estate planning seminars, which are open to the public. He offers two different seminars:

"Introduction to Estate Planning," a basic seminar covering wills, probate, planning for incapacity, revocable living trusts, and an introduction to estate and gift taxes;

" Planning to Minimize Estate Taxes," which focuses on planning ideas to reduce or eliminate gift and estate taxes, including bypass trusts and other planning ideas for married couples, use of the gift tax annual exclusion, and life insurance and gifts to charities.

The seminars are presented at the author's office on a rotating basis every third Friday of the month (except December). Contact the author for a schedule of seminars or to register.

You may contact the author at:

200 Willamette Oaks Building
6720 SW Macadam Avenue
Portland, Oregon 97219
Tel: (503) 245-0894
Fax: (503) 245-1562
E-mail: rcj@rcjlaw.com
Website: www.rcjlaw.com